OVERCOMING THE BITTERNESS OF WAR

OVERCOMING
THE BITTERNESS OF
WAR

ISATU BOYCE

Printed in the United States of America

Softcover ISBN: 978-1-964953-16-8
E-book ISBN: 978-1-964953-15-1
Library of Congress Control Number 2025900760

Edited by Erin Dionne
Prepared for Publication by Kathy J Perry of Chickadee Words, LLC
Cover & Interior Design by Principal Publishing

Contents

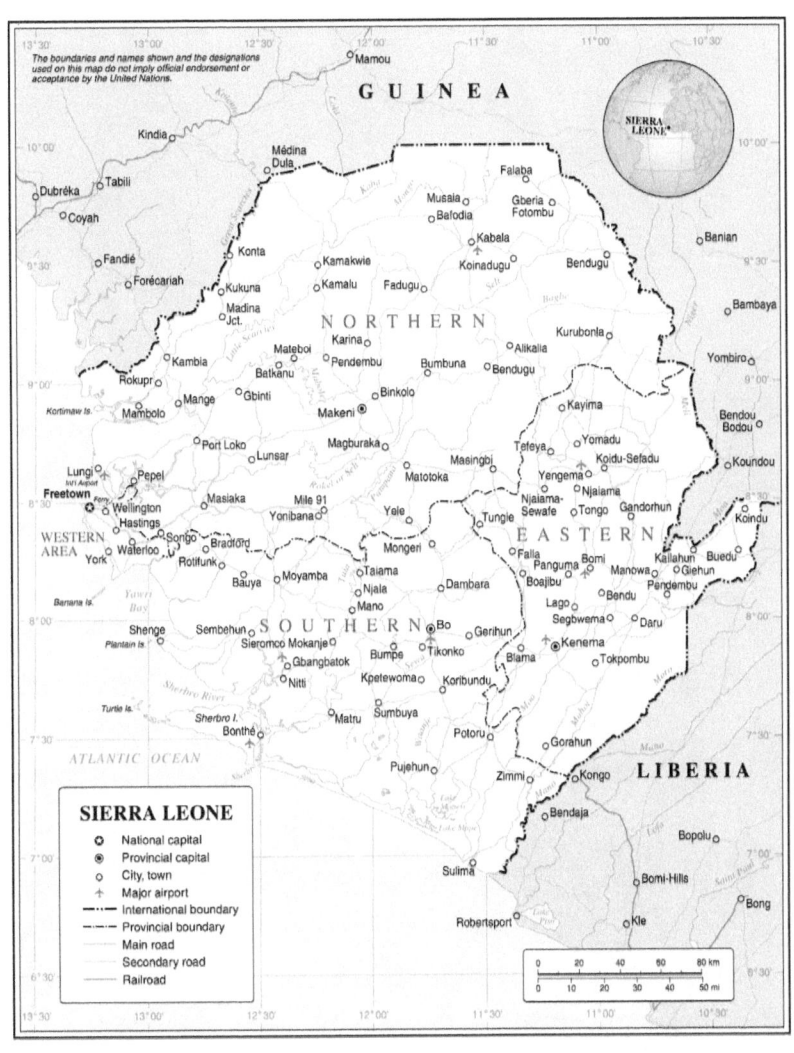

From OnTheWorldMap.com:

https://ontheworldmap.com/sierra-leone/sierra-leone-political-map.html

A Brief Overview of Sierra Leone

A Brief History ~

My country lays on the southwest coast of west Africa and is bordered by Liberia to the south. It has a population of around 7,075,641. Sierra Leone was explored by the Portuguese back in 1462, as they sailed down the coast of west Africa. They named it Sierra Leone or "lion's head", because its mountain resembles the head of a lion. It was claimed by the British as a crown colony from 1808 to 1961, when it was given its independence.

The capital city is Freetown and is the largest in Sierra Leone. The British named it that, after they freed many slaves. With beaches along our coastline, our men fish and boat a lot. Fruit trees and vegetation are valuable resources, too.

At first, I lived in a peaceful, small village, Moyamba, Sierra Leone, West Africa. Moyamba lay east of Freetown—about a day trip away. My first language was Temne. The country's many small villages each had a different tongue and religion, but all are brought together by one language: Krio, a broken English language. Krio was developed by the Krio people after being freed from slavery. These people were descendants of free African American slaves who settled in the western area of Sierra Leone after 1820.

Religion ~

The majority of Sierra Leone's people are Muslim (about 80%). Christianity is second.

Currency ~

One U.S. Dollar equals 22,705 Sierra Leone Leones. For perspective, this would feed you both lunch and dinner. Twenty U.S. dollars goes a long way!

Time & Weather ~

Time in Sierra Leone is the same as London time. We have calendars, but few clocks or watches. There are primarily two seasons: rainy and dry. Because the climate is tropical, it gets hot and humid. Used to the heat, I didn't suffer from the humidity. Temperatures can rise above 100° or sink to about 75°. That's very cold and many people get sick during this time.

Driving ~

Drivers stay on the right side of a one-lane road. It's pretty loud from all the cars honking and pulling to one side to pass each other. Some parts of the road are rough—very bumpy and dusty.

Food ~

Almost all our food has some type of spicy kick to it. It's full-flavored. I think food that's called sweet has some type of spice in it, because Sierra Leoneans don't care for the traditional sweet. We like more savory food. As a child, I don't remember craving anything sweet—except frozen yogurt. I think I liked it because it was cold and crunchy and I enjoyed it. We mostly ate starchy foods and no processed food whatsoever. We usually cooked what we grew or caught, so all our food is fresh from the ocean or the farm.

Housing in Moyamba ~

Our house wasn't large, but it was big enough for us—a family of four. It had two bedrooms, one window, and one door.

We had no plumbing, so no bathroom or shower inside. Those were outside along with our kitchen.

The house was made of red clay dirt, as were our beds. We'd put a mattress on the bed to make it soft and comfortable.

My dad had built it with help from friends. Because it was made of clay, we had a dusty floor to sweep often and keep clean. Sometimes we put a mat on the floor to hold down the dust.

The roof was thatched with palm leaves. When it rained, we stayed dry, except for a possible drip or two.

It didn't have many furnishings inside, but we did have a little clay stove in the corner inside to cook food, just in case it rained.

We had no electricity, so we used lamps for light. No air conditioning and no heat. If it was hot, we'd open the door or the window. If it was cold, we'd close them and make a fire in the clay stove to warm up the place, but we still had to open the window to let out the smoke.

Music ~

Music in my country is unique. Sierra Leoneans love to dance to reggae and tribal music. As a child, I remember we always sang songs that went with the games we played. And, each song had a story related to the game we played, which made it fun. Everyone got a chance to sing and make the song the way they wanted to make it.

Some would even put on a show to make it look like they are crying, but they are not. It could get dramatic at times, but we really weren't serious. We were just having fun. Of all the music in my country, I love reggae best because it's relaxing and makes you think about the meaning of life.

Moyamba, Sierra Leone

Life was beautiful when I was about five. I had no worries. But then again, I was just a little girl.

Fatmata, my sister, who was some years older than me, labored with my parents. My dad, Alimamy Kargbo, farmed. Every morning he rose early and took my sister out to the fields. Her job was to protect the crops from animals like snakes, monkeys, wild goats, wild pigs and an occasional lion, while my father cut down some trees for more space to grow food.

He grew peanuts, onions, garlic, peppers, rice, cucumbers, tomatoes, lima, pinto, black, and green beans, peas, squash, zuchinni, watermelon, casava, sweet potatoes, and pineapples. Also, we fished from a lake nearby and caught catfish and shrimp.

I helped my mom, Kadiatu Koroma, prepare food and then deliver it to my dad, my sister, and other workers on our farm. When they finished the meal, Mom, Fatmata, and I cleaned up and went home. Then we fetched some water, which took 30 minutes back and forth—an hour of walking with a heavy load on our heads, backs, and shoulders. But because of my size, I carried less weight.

But I felt sorry for family members that did heavy lifting, especially my dad. At the end of every day, he was covered in dirt and sweat and moved slowly. Some days, he seemed defeated. But when he brought in the crops, he was proud. A master farmer, he excelled with the growing of crops, and he worked hard at it. Mom was a master supporter of him and of mothering my sister and I. Since they started the family, this was the life our parents prepared us for.

I admired my parents' strength and hoped one day to be like my mom. In serving my dad, she made sure everything was ready for him when he came home from a long, hard-working day. His food was prepared and the house was clean and peaceful. They never fought or caused us worry. We all enjoyed health and happiness.

One day, my sister and I checked on the crops in the field. We found a huge snake, jumped over it, and ran as fast as possible. It slithered off as fast as we did. When we got home, we told our parents about the snake. Dad was so mad because Fatmata wasn't supposed to take me. I never accompanied my sister again in the fields.

My parents decided I had reached school age. One day, mom registered me for school. It didn't appear promising—dry and sad. I didn't want to go but mom dragged me, screaming, all the way to school. School was just as bad as I assumed it was—depressing. All day, I thought about how my mom would be preparing food to take to my dad. And how my mom and sister would fetch water without me. I just didn't want to be there. The day lasted forever—everything moved slowly. I couldn't wait to go home to my family and hear all about dad's day. He always had some fine stories to tell. What did my sister encounter in the field today? What stew did mom make for the workers? Would there be any left for me?

After school ended, I was so happy to leave that I ran home with no plan to return. Home at last, my day brightened. Everyone talked about their day except me. I didn't want to talk about being dragged to school against my will, so I sat quietly and enjoyed my family and the warm fire between us. I didn't want my bad day to mess it up.

At night, we all sat outside around the fire while the grownups told stories of how the leopard got their spots and why they were afraid of fire. Also, they told one about the spider and baboon: why the spider had a big stomach and why the inside of the baboon's hands were pink and many, many more stories. Some were scary, some were so funny, but these stories had a life lesson behind them. Our parents used stories to teach us about life.

Growing up in the village was a different life. The men of the village worked hard every day, too, but they hunted to provide for their families. Their lives were always at risk of being attacked by wild animals like lions and snakes, but they loved it. Something about it made them think they were more manly.

Our backyard was like a forest. Sometimes wild animals showed up from time to time, but usually, nothing scary like lions. We saw lots of monkeys and wild chickens we called bushfowl.

We had lots of fruit trees as well. Sometimes, I reached up and picked fruit from the shorter trees. It was like I was in the middle of the Garden of Eden. I was so blessed to wake up every morning to such beauty.

Life was wonderful, and I had friends to play with. I had everything I needed and loved my life—everything but school. School was still not my thing. But my parents thought I should have a good education, so they threatened to send me away to a better school. Fatmata was more help to them, I guess. I might have been in the way. I thought they were joking until one day a visitor showed up.

It was a lady I don't remember ever seeing before. She came to talk to my parents about something. The whole time they talked, she kept looking at me. I didn't like her at all. Her smile looked like she was up to something and I didn't trust her. She talked for far too long. I just wanted her to leave already. Then mom called me to come meet her. Mom said, "Isatu, meet your aunt. Her name is Dankey."

What? I said to myself. I had more family members? This lady looks nothing like the other relatives. I asked, "Why hasn't she come before?"

Mom said, "She's come from the city to pick up some supplies for her business: rice, fruits, vegetables, and palm oil. She owns a nice market in the city and she has a little girl, just two years older than you. And she wants you to go live with her where you can attend a better school, like her little girl, and be able to become anything you want when you grow up."

I ran and sat on my mom's lap and whispered to her that I didn't want to go with my aunt. I wanted to stay home with her, dad, and my sister. She said little after that. When it was time for my aunt to leave, my parents gave her a large bag full of rice, lots of fruits and vegetables, and some oils for free. Then they said goodbye.

Thrilled I wasn't going with her, my goodbye was cheerful. I got to stay with my parents and she returned home without me. I asked mom if my aunt would ever come back. She said, "Yes, but not for a long time."

About two months later, I had improved at school—and had grown a little stronger. Now, I helped a little around the house and was so proud of myself. I wanted my parents to realize I had grown old enough to do things, like my sister, so they wouldn't send me away. Some days I even stayed until school was dismissed! Although they appeared happy with my enthusiasm, their faces hid something from me. I wanted to ask, but was afraid to. I just left it like that.

As night approached, something wasn't right. While I played with my friends, I tried to have fun, but something stopped me. I laughed with my friends one minute, and the next minute, I looked at them with sadness. It was all too much for me to handle, so I went in for bed. The whole night I clung to my parents, sleeping with them. I didn't want anyone to take me away from them.

Morning came and the feelings I'd had last night had passed. I was happy to start a new day. Then mom told me I wouldn't be helping them today because my aunt was coming to take me with her. My parents gave me no reason for this. I felt like someone just took my heart out and ran with it. Everything drained out of me. I wanted to run, but I had nowhere to go! I wailed—like someone I loved very much had just died.

Half the village heard me, so some neighbors even came by to find out what was happening. Watching mom pack the few things I had in a little bag made me feel unwanted.

I pleaded with her. "Please Mom and Dad, don't let me go. I need you and my sister. I promise to work hard and be good. Please, I want to stay with my family." I cried so hard it hurt. Mom held me close to her and rocked me while dad held my hand. My sister stood over me and spoke encouragements to me. She told me I'm only going for a year of school. And if I don't like it, they will come for me. She added they would visit me a lot and I might visit on Christmas. I felt a little better because of all the promises made.

The next thing that happened was my dad packing the truck with my belongings and lots of food for me. The truck was full, but Dad came out with two chickens to send with me for pets. I knew my parents and my sister loved me. I saw it in their eyes and in the way they acted.

Figuring that maybe there was a reason for all this, I obeyed and did what they wanted for me even though I felt like I died inside. My parents hugged me tight, my sister didn't want to let go of me, and my friends cried and waved goodbye. Then the driver Aunt Dankey had hired pulled away with herself and me in the back with all the stuff. Sick and afraid, I screamed, "Mama, Papa, sister, please don't forget me!"

To Freetown

I'm sick and afraid. Being the first time I rode in a moving thing, I grew sicker the further we went. Then, I threw up, which forced the driver to pull over and clean up the truck and me. I'd cried and screamed for so long my voice was gone. Still sick as we continued the long, bumpy drive, I tried to sleep to avoid the ache inside and dozed off at last.

I dreamt I was playing with my friends. My mom cooked with my sister. My dad walked home from work. I ran to meet him and we walked into the house, filled with the yummy smells from the food we would eat. A bump in the road jostled me out of my pleasant dream and I resumed my hoarse crying.

It wasn't an ordinary bump after all. Our driver pulled over to check the tire and found it had blown. We all had to climb off the truck, and it took about an hour before the driver had fixed the tire and we were on our way again. We stopped at almost every single little town we passed to pick up and drop off people, making the trip long. There were so many crowded in the back of the truck, it was uncomfortable.

After a few stops, the truck struggled to move at the speed it should because of all the weight it carried. So, some people had to jump off and wait for other transportation. We had only two more stops before we arrived at our destination: Freetown, the coastal capital of Sierra Leone.

As we entered this new town, the driver shouted complaints about the number of bridges he had to cross on small roads. The first bridge was a high one, but the water rose to almost the height of its road. Because of the roughness of the bridge's surface, the loads on the truck, which included my aunt, and I, shifted from one side to the other.

I'd never been so frightened for my life. My aunt took me in her arms and held me tight. I cried. I didn't want to go on this trip to the capital city in the first place and now we were fighting for our lives to even make it. How would my family handle the bad news that their little girl never made it to where they were going—all because of a bad bridge no one had fixed?

Just when I thought we were safe, we came upon another crazy one. The heavy truck got stuck in the swampy, muddy approach to the bridge. All passengers had to climb off the truck and walk across that part. Thank goodness, the water wasn't too high here, or we'd all sink. But we made it. Who knew you had to go through a death trap to travel to Freetown?

This trip was the longest I'd ever been so still. I began to fidget. Normally, this child of five years would play or work outside all day. As we entered the last village, the road smoothed out, and the ride grew more comfortable.

My aunt, whose name I learned was Dankey, told me about Freetown in my language—how her little girl, my cousin, Beria, couldn't wait to play with me and how life would be better for me. She would sign me up for school and I'd learn to speak Krio. Her promises sounded good, but I still missed my home and my family.

We arrived in Freetown late in the evening and the air smelled of the nutty scents of roasted corn and cassava people had prepared for their dinners. Vendors crowded the street, cars honked, some people fought, and others laughed. The noise, the different languages, and the diverse looks of people were brand new to me.

Speaking of diversity, I didn't resemble either Dankey or her child, as I would learn. My skin is lighter, and my nose has a different shape. Some people stared at me because they could tell I was new by the way I appeared and spoke—even by the way I moved. They were quicker. I moved like I had nowhere to go—too slow for them.

At last, the truck stopped at the Freetown marketplace. We got off and Dankey's daughter, husband, and a boy greeted us. Thank goodness they brought us rice and stew to eat because we hadn't eaten anything for the whole trip. Starved, I devoured every bit of this food.

That night, we played some games, which was hard for me because of the language difference. But they tried hard to welcome me. I almost forgot I wasn't with my family until it was time for bed. Then, trying hard not to make noise, I cried again because I miss them so much. Crying in silence, I just wanted my mom to hold me. But I was too far away from them.

After my long silent cry, I slept. When I woke up, my cousin had already gone to school and my aunt was setting up her business for the day in the marketplace. My uncle had left for work. After eating breakfast, I sat with my aunt as she taught me how to sell stuff in the market. Boring.

Across from the marketplace, a school let out the students for their lunches and games. It looked like such fun—much better than the school back in my home village. We didn't have uniforms. We just went as we were. This school was big and fancy. The uniforms were fancy; the children looked fancy in them, and they had their lunch boxes and backpacks, nice high socks, nice black shoes, and their hair was nicely done. Everything looked just perfect about them. Maybe one day I would look like and be happy like them. Would this be the school I attend? Might I have the chance to be like them? I hoped so.

But at the marketplace, our day had been long and hot, sitting under the sun. Business was okay. One minute we'd have lots of buyers. The next minute, a few would stop. Some just walked by without looking.

Soon, school would be dismissed and my cousin would come home. Would she tell me about her day? I thought she didn't go to the fancy school closer to the market because she attended a school a long way away with older children. Her uniform was just as nice, though.

We had a few more people come by who bought lots of rice and oil. They needed these things to prepare their dinners. Then the school bells rang. All the children ran out to either meet their parents who picked them up, or walk home by themselves. My cousin ran toward us and hugged me tight. She missed me like I did her!

Beria showed me what she did at school today. I understood nothing, but it was fun watching her. Tall and thin, Beria resembled both of her parents. She had her mom's dark complexion, and her dad's oval face and long arms and legs. We walked home together so she could change from her school uniform into play clothes.

We returned to the market, which was only a few minutes' walk from the house, and tended it while Dankey left to start dinner. Beria runs the business like her mother, but her mother didn't let her sell large items; only small ones. I had to fetch my aunt if someone wanted a gallon of oil. While waiting for customers, she taught me how to say things in Krio, like counting and doing basic stuff like that. She taught well.

Dankey came and got us for dinner. Afterward, we returned to the market to bring everything back in for the night. We washed up and got ready for the evening games with kids who came over. Some games reminded me of my village and the games I used to play back home with friends.

I remembered how my parents would sit and watch us play the same games they played as children. One of them is traditional: all the girls stood at one end and the boys stood at the other end. We sang a song and one boy would pick a girl he liked and so on to the next boy. Sometimes a brief fight broke out if one boy picked a girl another boy might like. But all the boys loved each other and the girls just wanted a boy to come for them.

But tonight, I played a new game, far from home. Beria set up four chairs, but there were five of us. So, we sang a song, walked around the chairs, and when the music stopped, we all had to find a seat. If you didn't have a chair, you were out. It was a fun and simple game, but I wasn't able to sit in a chair and found myself on the floor a lot. We played and laughed hard until it was bedtime and everyone went to their places.

I lay on the bed with Beria. It wasn't made of clay, but was a mattress on box springs set in a frame so it was off the floor. Back home, so many creatures filled the nights with their sounds. Tonight, I had trouble sleeping for the quietness. The next day we repeated the same things again: me at the market with Dankey, and Beria at school. The next night, we played different games. I taught them my games, and they loved them so much.

After several weeks, my Krio strengthened and my marketplace skills improved. Every night, my cousin taught me what she learned from school.

A month later, Dankey signed me up for school, at last! I was excited about it until she gave me the uniform I was to wear. Disappointed, I thought I might attend the school by the market. Instead, she signed me up for a Muslim school out of respect for my parents, who were Muslim. I just wanted to go to a regular school, like Beria, but she didn't listen.

My new uniform came with a pant and a head wrap, which I loved very much. It fit snugly and was my favorite color: green. It also kept the sun from beating down on my head and neck. The next day, I'd start school rather than sit at the marketplace all day. Now, I'd be one of the many kids in school learning and doing school stuff. For my first day, I wasn't afraid. I was excited as I put on my uniform. I felt and looked good.

Since Beria was at a different school than me, we couldn't walk together. Dankey walked me to school the first day to show me the way. But, she told me I had to remember the way back as I'd be alone after school.

She gave me lunch money. No lunchbox, no backpack. I just carried my one book and one pencil. No long pretty socks, or black fancy shoes. Just sandals. I cared little about not having any of that stuff. It would have been nice to dress in a fancy uniform, but I was happy to be going to school. My aunt started me in grade one.

My class held about thirty children—all clean and ready to learn. I sat by a girl, tinier than me, who shook with fear of her first day of school. As soon as the teacher entered the classroom, we stood up to greet her. As we said the greeting, something dripped, like water. I glanced up at my new buddy beside me. She cried because she wet herself. I thought I was afraid, but she was worse than I was. Our classroom had a dusty cement floor, so I helped cover it up so no one would see what happened. But the teacher knew and told her it would dry and not to worry about it.

The bell rang. Why was the bell ringing just as we got to school? Is it over already? We didn't learn or eat lunch. I collected my school things, but my teacher told me we didn't need them. We were going out for the morning prayer and our national anthem. The teacher said the bell rings three times each day: the prayer bell, the lunch bell, and the last one at dismissal.

We stood in line by grade level for about fifteen minutes while the head teacher of the school walked around to make sure every student was well-dressed, hair fixed nicely, had proper shoes, and an ironed uniform. Failure to meet any requirement resulted in being sent home.

At least I got things right the first day because I didn't understand there would be an inspection. Thank goodness they gave warnings on the first day. Back in my village, the teachers didn't care about how you dressed as long as you had clothes on your body. I hoped I could follow all these demands. Not only were you sent home if you failed, you got spankings for not being clean, or having messy hair or dirty nails. And you couldn't paint those because they had to see your natural nails.

After the head teacher finished talking, we sang our morning song and were dismissed to our classes with our teachers. As we entered the classroom, our teacher gave each of us a slate and a piece of chalk. We started learning! I already knew my letters and numbers from Beria's teaching,

I was excited, until I found out we were going to learn a different way. We wouldn't be learning in Krio, but in Arabic. I knew how to pray in Arabic, but not write. The only reason I could pray in Arabic was because I always followed my mom when she went to the mosque to pray. This would be harder than I thought! I couldn't even speak proper Krio and next I had to learn how to write and read in Arabic.

As I wrote the new characters, I found I liked the smoothness of it. It wasn't as hard as I expected. My disappointment disappeared. After all, I could still learn to write in Krio from my cousin.

When the lunch bell rang, all the kids ran out with their lunches. Some, like me, brought money for lunch. I bought fish, bread, and cold water. I ate and played with my new friend outside. Her uniform had dried and you couldn't tell it was ever wet.

After lunch, we stood in line again to make sure all of us were still present. That afternoon was sunny and hot and the children sweated. The teachers had stayed in the shade, so the sun hadn't bothered them. But couldn't they see us melting away? Our uniforms lacked ventilation. Instead, they trapped in the heat.

Thankfully, everyone was present, so the teachers dismissed us to our classrooms to complete our daily work. I concentrated on my work, so the time went by quickly and I ignored the sweat.

The dismissal bell rang and this school day was over. Why didn't the time fly like this when I sat with Dankey in the marketplace? Selling in the marketplace was boring. Walking home scared me because I remembered little of the road, so I took a wrong turn and ended up in an unfamiliar place. Why wouldn't Dankey meet me? I continued walking and ended up where I started.

Frustrated, I returned to the school and reported to my teacher. I told her I'd forgotten the way home, but I thought I lived close. She walked home with me and as we approached the house, Beria came toward us. I thanked my teacher for helping me and ran to meet my cousin.

As we walked home together, we chatted about our days. My first day of school went well. They didn't send me home for not having the right things, so it was a fine first day.

School Days

Some weeks later, I returned from school to an unhappy Aunt Dankey. I asked her what was wrong. She said she wasn't able to sell much and that she needed some help with the business. Then she asked me to change clothes and walk around the market to sell some things.

Why was she asking me to do this? Her daughter came home sooner than me. Why didn't Aunt Dankey ask *her* for help? I was tired, hungry, and speechless. She hadn't even asked me about my school day. I wanted to say no, but didn't think I should, so I just agreed, which made her happy. Glad this changed her attitude, I changed my clothes and filled a tray with onions.

While Beria did her homework, I put the load on my head and went off to sell. I guessed her schooling was way more important than mine. I had homework too, but mine had to wait.

It didn't take me long to sell all but three onions. Aunt Dankey was happy my tray was almost empty and told me she would sign me up for a study class every day after dinner, so I didn't have to miss out on my schoolwork. I would try to keep her happy if I could and was thankful for the study class. I thought If I did good and stayed on her good side, she might let me visit my family.

The saddest times for me were in the morning, as I got ready for the day, and at bedtime every night. I always missed my family. I couldn't go to them, so all I did was obey. Would Dankey allow me to visit them for Christmas?

So, that night was different. I had a lot of things to do before I played with my friends. I had to shower, wash my uniform, do my homework, and iron my other uniform. By the time I finished, I was tired.

All Beria and I could do was share stories with the neighbor kids. I told them one of my favorite stories from my sister about a fool who tried to find water. He couldn't decide which road to take: the long one or the short one. So he took the long one. He was almost there when he changed his mind and went back so he could go the short way. I loved this story because it made everyone laugh. And because it calmed me down and made me think about the world I live in.

The first few weeks of school went well. My Arabic writing was stronger because of the evening study class. I loved the place I went for my lessons. It was in a bakery shop with a tall fruit tree out front. The wonderful scent of fresh-baked bread hung in the air. If I was hungry, the baker gave us some bread and butter. Because the bread was still warm, the butter melted quickly and made the bread ten times better. So, I loved the class even more.

Also, the baker let me eat from the tree if I wanted. I looked forward to this class, even after my long day at school, selling things in the market for two hours, and taking all the market back home. It was worth it.

It took me five rounds to pack the market. I hardly got together with Beria anymore, so I had to do everything by myself. Sometimes, she didn't even come home after school. I worried about her, so I asked my aunt about it.

She said, "She is staying at her brother's."

"What?" I asked. "My cousin has brothers?"

Dankey explained, "My daughter has three older brothers. Your uncle was married before marrying me. He has three sons from his first marriage, but his first wife died from malaria. The boys, now in their 20s and 30s, live independently. The oldest one is a doctor and the other two have good-paying jobs. They're all doing well for themselves."

Things made sense. Because of what happened to my uncle's first wife, he became a medicine man. That's why he practiced with different plant roots: to come up with a medicine that can cure malaria and much more. This is also why his oldest son became a doctor: to help people. My uncle was ten years older than Aunt Dankey and Beria was their only child together. Now, Beria was pretty much living with her older brother and his wife and two children. She only visited Aunt Dankey's house.

But the thing is, Beria didn't want to live with her brother, even though she loved him. She just wanted to be around me. But Aunt Dankey didn't think it was a good idea. I didn't understand why, but she said it was too much of a distraction. She claimed her daughter needed to focus more on her schoolwork. With us together, Dankey thought her schoolwork suffered.

Now, every time my cousin visited, we played hard. I don't think Beria came home for her mom. I think she did it for her dad. Her brothers wanted her to visit to make sure their dad was doing well. The boys didn't enjoy being around my aunt that much because they rarely came to visit their father at the house. When they came, they stayed with him at the market where he sold his medicine.

My uncle didn't talk too much, but he always got into trouble with my aunt. Sometimes, he went out and came back home drunk and my aunt would beat him. I never understood the reason he appeared so helpless. I cried for him because he wasn't able to fight for himself.

Once, I came between them so she would stop hitting him. I got the hardest slap ever! By morning, my face had a mark and my uncle's face had some marks, too.

He glanced at me and smiled and said, "You were brave, but next time, don't get in the way and get hurt."

I asked. "Do you remember what happened last night?"

He told me everything. "I wasn't drunk, but every time I get home, she *thinks* I'm drunk and never believes me."

So, I asked him, "Where do you go every night?"

He said, "To my sister's house where I will drink, but I'm never drunk."

I asked, "Why do you let Dankey beat you and never fight back?"

He said, "Because she thinks I'm weak and do little. So, I let her do what she wants. After all, she doesn't love me anymore. The first time I met her, she loved me, but now she loves someone else. I don't think she knows I know about him."

My uncle continued. "He was my friend, but not anymore. He used to come and act like he came to chat with me, but the real reason was to visit her. I act like I don't notice, but I do. And, if that is who she wants, then she can go for him. I just can't fight for her love anymore. He is young and I'm an old fool. Who do you think she will go for? "

He smiled. "But enough about me. You need to do your job and prepare yourself for school. You don't want to be late and receive a beating from your teacher and sent back home."

Wow! Is that what happens to students for being late? Did I miss this announcement at school?

I got ready fast, took everything to the market, and waited for my aunt to come so I could go home and prepare for school. I didn't want to mess up my uniform, so I hadn't dressed for school first. My aunt was ten minutes late, so I moved even faster now and ran to the school fifteen minutes away.

I arrived only five seconds before the bell rang! My teacher was glad I made it and smiled. She was so beautiful when she smiled at me. She was kind to all her students and, since I had started school, I hadn't seen her spank or make anyone feel small or bad about themselves. And, some came to school with messy hair.

She would fix their hair before our morning prayer so they didn't get in trouble. Sometimes, we heard other children getting spankings and crying. It made me sad because I didn't have any idea what their spanking was for. Our class was one where no one cried—not because we were perfect, but because we had a teacher with a merciful heart.

I hoped and prayed the other children got a teacher like ours. Not every parent had money so their children could have nice shoes or endless supplies of uniforms. Not every parent braided super-nicely. If you wanted your hair to be extra-nice, some people paid braiders for that to happen. If their parents couldn't do any of this, teachers spanked their students at school. My aunt could afford to give me good shoes, hair braids, and buy me a new uniform. But did she want to do all that for me? No, I didn't think so.

She once told me if my shoes and uniform fell apart, she wouldn't buy a new one. I must try my best to keep it from ripping or getting stained. I couldn't do much to protect my shoes. They took a beating from the walk to school and back every day. For my hair, she gave up doing it. She did it only twice: the first day of school and the beginning of the second week of school.

So, every day I only put up my hair and tried to make it perfect. For my nails, I bit them to keep them short. For lunch, I no longer took money to school because Dankey said it was too expensive for me to do every day. I would have to eat after school. I was fine with that because I ate rice and stew for breakfast every day.

The first day I missed lunch was okay. I just thought about how much I would eat when I got home. The second day, my friend asked why I didn't have lunch. I lied and told her I forgot my money at home. The next day, I lied and said I wasn't hungry. Every day was a different story, until one day my teacher understood and gave me some money for lunch.

I was grateful for her generosity, but I didn't want her to waste her money on me. So, the next day, I took some money from my aunt's bag. It wasn't enough, but at least I could munch on something so no one felt sorry for me not having food at lunchtime. My teacher was happy seeing me eating, but my lunch didn't taste that good to me because I had to steal to have it. I felt guilty all the way home. I was sorry for what I did.

When I arrived home, I greeted my aunt, but she didn't answer. She asked one of her friends to mind the business for her and dragged me by the ear all the way to the house. She threw me on the ground and spanked me. I had never experienced such a beating in my life. When she was done, she asked me where her money was. I confessed I took it for lunch and she whipped me some more and told me I wouldn't be eating until the morning because of what I did.

The stolen money was not worth all the spanking or withholding of dinner from me, but it was the punishment for my actions. I wondered what my parents would have said about the spanking and punishment she gave me. Well, it didn't matter anymore. All I felt was the pain from the marks she gave me. My uniform was all dirty, so I took it off and soaked it in a bucket before I went to the market. I had little luck selling this time. I thought everyone saw the petty thief I was.

After working the market, I had to help make dinner, though I couldn't eat any of it. I thought I might be off that job, but, oh, no; I was still doing it, just not eating. This punishment was the worst. By the end of the evening, my stomach hurt and my body shook as I lay in bed. I cried, but didn't understand why. Was it because I missed my family that I hurt all over?

Was the world too much for me to understand? I didn't understand why my aunt went from fine to mad so quickly. How was my teacher so caring and merciful to her students and, next door, others showed no mercy?

I thought about how this world all came together. Was it made by someone that had a heart, like my teacher? Everything was so perfect when it rained. How did the water come down like that? And how did the sun shine and make everything so bright? And at night, so many shining stars.

Was the moon in charge of all the stars? Was it? After all, there's a face of a man wearing a crown on his head. Is he the one who made everything? He's so perfect. I still don't comprehend why I thought about all of this.

I just wanted to lie in bed, feel sorry for myself, and cry for my empty stomach. But my mind kept taking me places that were bigger than it could contain. As I dozed off, I dreamt I was in the village with my family. Everyone was so happy. My mom made my favorite food. I was happy— eating my bean stew, which Mom served over rice.

Church

My aunt woke me with a *SMACK* to my backside. Oh, no! Back to reality. My face must have appeared depressed because Dankey asked me, "Why were you crying last night?"

"I don't know," I said and then asked, "Who made the world?"

She said, "God."

"Is he the guy in the moon?"

Surprised, she said, "No. Would you like to come with us to church tomorrow and learn about Him?"

"Oh, yes!" They had never asked me if I wanted to come with them before. Was it was because my parents were Muslim and she didn't want to change who I was? Later that day she bought me a pretty dress and shoes to go with it. I was so excited! As I added them with my other five pieces of clothing, I wished the next day would come already so I could wear them and feel beautiful.

Since it was Saturday, school was out. This day seemed long because I had to be at the market all day, though that pleased my aunt. At least I didn't get in trouble. That night, the moon was full, and it was hard to make out the man in it. This time, it was more like another world in it, but it wasn't clear. I wanted to talk to the man in the moon. Did he only come when the moon was half-full? I wasn't sad, though, because the next day I would learn about him.

Sunday was beautiful. Not only did I go to church for the first time, I felt beautiful. And also, it was a day of rest for me: no market, no selling.

I even received more welcome news. My parents would come to visit next Saturday! We all dressed up for church, but my uncle dressed extra sharp today. We left early for the ten-minute walk to the church. I entered the place.

The church was large, and the sweet fragrance of clean people filled the air. Everyone smiled and greeted us with friendly faces. Beautiful choirs sang with so much power that people seemed like they were crying and singing at the same time. But it wasn't a sad cry. Something about it made me want to stay with them and experience their feelings. But all the children had to go to their classes.

When the leader called my name, my heart pounded. Frightened, I worried he might ask me something I couldn't answer. But, no, he was just introducing me to the other children. Everyone was nice and friendly. Our leader opened up a book that he called his Bible and said he would read about faith today. He read about a man who had the power to heal sick and broken people.

A man came to him and asked, "Will you heal my sick child?"

The man with power asked, "Where is the child?"

The man answered, "The child is at home and very sick. I know you're a busy man, but if you just say the word, it will be well."

The master looked at him and said, "Because of your faith, the child is well now."

So the man left with a heart full of joy because he believed everything the master had said.

Our teacher told us that was the end of the lesson today. But I didn't want him to be done with the story. I wanted more. I wanted to understand more about this man that had a power like that. So, I asked, "Is there more to that story?"

He said, "Yes. If you want to learn more, you must come every Sunday."

I was so happy, I couldn't even wait for next Sunday to come already.

The teacher dismissed our class to go the bigger service for communion. This was only for the grown-ups. They lined up, one row at a time, to go by the pastor to eat something like bread and to drink from a tall glass. Everyone was drinking out of the same glass, which I thought was weird. I turned to my uncle and asked, "Why are the children not allowed to have some?"

He said, "It's only for people who understand the meaning behind it."

I asked, "What does it mean?"

He said, "The bread is the body of the man who died for us. His name is Jesus. The drink in the cup is the blood he shed, so we do this to remind us he loves us and that we love him, too."

I didn't understand this, and I was annoying my uncle with all of my questions. I'd wait until next Sunday to ask my Sunday School teacher about the man named Jesus. I liked Sunday most of all the days of the week. I think this day was my favorite.

Back in my village, we didn't celebrate Sunday like they did here in the city. It's like its own special holiday. Lots of people took it as a resting day, but some didn't care about it. If my aunt cared so much for this one day of the week, there must be a reason behind it.

But I'd save my questions for my Sunday School teacher next week. After all, I had many, many questions and I didn't want to be thrown out of the house for asking them when we returned home.

I felt different. Now my life had a little more meaning. I had one day of the week to look forward to and I got to learn about something new and exciting. At church, I didn't worry about getting spanked if I didn't have the answers to questions and no one judged me for how I dressed. I was safe in that place.

Having to do less work after church was fun. I filled up all the containers with water and cleaned the house, washed my uniforms, and got them ready for school the next day. I tried to do everything ahead of time so I'd have plenty of time to play later with friends. Since Beria was with us today, it was more fun to play and tell scary stories.

In the morning, we both would go to school. Afterward, she would go off to her brother's house for the rest of the week. Every time I got used to having her around, she'd leave again. Sometimes she didn't even come home for the weekend. I wish she just stayed with us. Having her around made me less afraid of my aunt. And less alone.

I couldn't wait to tell my family everything I'd been doing and learning when they visited. Of all the weeks I'd been here, this had been the fastest because of the excitement running through my veins.

Friday, my aunt told me what to say to my parents, like all the things she's doing for me and how wonderful school is. She didn't want me to talk too much. But it's hard not to talk too much when I haven't seen them for a few months now. Why was I practicing what to say to my parents? Was Dankey afraid I'd tell them about the spankings and punishment?

I cared little about what she wanted me to say. I just wanted to see my parents. All day long, my aunt was kind to me and laughed at things I said or did at night. It was hard to fall asleep for my excitement. What would they say when they saw me? Would they say I've grown? Would they want to take me back with them? Or would this be my forever home? Oh, the thought of that last part laid heavy on my heart. At last, I relaxed and let my tiredness take me away.

Saturday morning, I woke up excited for the day. I took out the market and came home to fill up the containers with water. I cleaned up the house and took a pleasant, cold shower. Then Aunt Dankey and I went to the market and waited for my parents to arrive. Time stood still. Impatiently, I watched every bus that came up our street. Did my aunt confuse the dates? I waited and waited until no more buses came. Hungry, I went to the house to eat lunch.

Then Beria ran towards me with a wide smile. Breathing heavily, she said, "Your parents are here. They are here! And they brought lots of things with them."

My first thought was that they were here to stay, or perhaps they brought the rest of my things and I was to stay here for the rest of my life. But, then again, I didn't remember leaving anything behind. I didn't remember having any more than I brought when I left with my aunt.

Back at the market, I couldn't believe my eyes. I hugged and kissed my parents for a long time. I couldn't believe they were finally here. Was this real or was I dreaming? If I was dreaming, when I woke up I was gonna cry until my aunt took me back to my village.

I pinched myself and screamed, jumped for joy, and waited to see if it was a dream. If it was, my aunt would slap it right out of me. But no slap came. All I got was a crowd looking at me.

I was so happy I wanted to take them and show them the house, but my aunt told me to wait for all of us to go together. Today, we would close the market early so we could go home and cook for my parents and talk more.

My family was amazed that I spoke a new language. My sister wanted me to teach her how to speak Krio. We laughed a lot. I even tried to teach my parents, which was even funnier. They tried so hard. I told my sister she'd have to teach me how to braid hair, since I was helping her speak Krio.

Let's just say it was easier to learn a language than to learn how to braid. It wasn't easy for me and we only had one day. It wasn't enough, but I loved the time I got to spend with her.

After dinner, I opened all the things my parents brought me. There was so much food, including my favorite dessert, canya, made from powdered rice, peanut butter, and sugar. I shared it with my friends and they loved it, too.

That night went so well, I didn't want it to end. But the next day, my family would return to their village. At story time, my sister was the storyteller. It was fun listening to her. I'd always remember this night. I wished she could stay with me to make it easier, but my parents needed her because she was old enough to help with the farm.

It didn't seem fair that she was in Moyamba and I was here. I just wanted us to grow up together, but I doubted that would happen. Maybe one day we would. I'd just hope for that for now.

Sunday morning, I woke up, happy to see my family again. We ate breakfast and then went for a walk. I wanted to show them around the area.

When we got back home, they packed their stuff. Sadness crept in again. It hurt every time I said goodbye. I'm terrible at this. I wished I didn't have to, but I might have to say goodbye a lot. Depressed, I stood in the street and waved until I couldn't see them anymore. Even then, I hoped the car would turn around and come back. But it never did.

Tears welled up in my eyes and my heart was heavy with pain all over again. I hated goodbyes and, to top it all, Aunt Dankey told me Beria was going to stay with her brother permanently. I didn't think the day could get any worse, but it did. Now, I'd be here forever by myself.

In addition, families had been steadily moving out of the compound I lived in. Almost all my friends had moved except one boy, Ali, whose dad knew the landlord well. He made a decent amount of money, so he paid rent at the proper time.

Nobody ever stayed for too long. Every time I made new friends, they'd leave. It got hard to know anyone. I was afraid to make friends. Some families that moved in had smaller children—none my age. Some families had no children at all and were cranky. Those ended up moving out faster than they moved in. Nobody ever meant to stay at those empty houses except for Ali, his dad, and my aunt and I.

Ali shared the same name as my younger brother, whom I learned about through a messenger, so I tried to treat him as if he was. But after a few weeks, he became mean and attacked me like I did something to him.

He wouldn't let me pass through to my house until I begged him. I did this for a few times until I got sick of it. When he did it again, I fought him. Ali won the first fight, but the second fight I won. He won a third. I won a fourth. I finally told him I wouldn't fight anymore, and that I'd tell his dad if he blocked me again.

Ali stopped me again the next day, so I told his dad what had been happening. His dad talked to him, but must not have said much, because the next day he was at it again. Because his dad wasn't home, he acted even worse this time. We started fighting again. I was winning because he wasn't fighting back. So, I stopped. He went and brought me some cold water and rice. I was hungry, so I ate. Then we both started laughing! He said, smiling, "I guess we are friends, again."

Unsettled

The next week was long and depressing, since we missed church Sunday because my Muslim parents visited. School was going well and almost finished. I'd done a good job and deserved to move up a grade the next year. But Aunt Dankey had been talking to me about working the market more. Wouldn't my success make her happy? If I failed, she would have more reason to take me out of school to help her.

I hoped I'd pass all my classes so Dankey would be proud of me and let me continue school. But she was very stressed, which rubbed off on me somehow. I wished she wasn't. It saddened me because I didn't know how to make her happy. To try, most times I did things before she asked.

Some days she was fine, but on others she would beat me—hard. I was upset because I didn't know who I'd see. Even when she smiled, I didn't know if she was ok. It felt lonely with just me and her at the house now.

I didn't see my uncle that much anymore, either. One Sunday came and my uncle was nowhere to be found. My aunt stayed home, so I was the only one that went to church.

The leader went over last Sunday's lesson, which was about trust. The story was that Jesus' disciples were on a boat and saw someone walking on the water. They were afraid, so one of them, Peter, called out, "Lord, if that is you, call me to you." So, he called. Peter went to him because he trusted him. When he realized he was walking on water, he became afraid. But because he trusted him, he believed Jesus would save him if he sank.

I loved this story so much because Jesus is so powerful. He can even walk on water! I couldn't even walk on normal ground without tripping and falling. I was so hungry, not for food, but for the stories of this wonderful man called Jesus. The story was so real. It felt like it was happening now, in front of my face.

I made a vow to attend church, with or without my aunt or uncle, just to hear more of these stories. Since I was a baby, my parents had told me stories. I grew up with stories as an important part of my life. Stories taught us basic life lessons and also made us laugh. But the stories Jesus told made me want to believe in something I can't see but know is there. It gave me hope to understand something good will come, even when things look bad.

I used faith in my life by believing that my aunt would smile more. Maybe she would be free from whatever was keeping happiness from her and stop beating her husband. I truly believed, one day, I would be free from her and return to my parents.

I was tired of being beaten for things I never did. Sometimes she would beat me hard and then rub hot pepper on my skin. I wanted Jesus to save me from her. Would he reach out his hand to me like he did for Peter? I wanted him to save me from drowning. Things were so hard with Aunt Dankey. Apparently, I did nothing right.

On the day I received my report card, I came in third in my class out of thirty. Aunt Dankey said, "This report couldn't be correct because you are not that smart. You should be in the market with me and, since your cousin is smarter, she should keep going to school instead of you."

I cried and cried, but it did no good. The only thing I got from crying was a big headache. The saddest part was that she wasn't sorry about it. She didn't care how I felt. Instead, she talked about the new job she planned for me. She finally seemed happy. Could my school attendance have caused her misery?

After only one week, my new job exhausted me. I had to wake up at five o'clock each morning to sell freshly made homemade soap before the sun came out.

Then, I set up the market for my aunt, got water for the house, and found a place to wash clothes.

After washing, I went straight to the market to sell some rice. Most of the time, I didn't have lunch and, since I didn't eat breakfast, I got very weak.

Throughout the day, I didn't have time to tell stories anymore, plus new kids made fun of how my aunt treated me. So, I felt lonely and afraid that these newcomers would beat me up like my aunt, and that no one would fight for me.

I found myself alone, looking at the night sky. The sky had so many friends—all of them twinkling so bright. Why didn't I have any friends anymore?

Sometimes I feared making new friends because I worried my aunt might beat them, too. I didn't feel like a kid anymore. Now, at seven years old, I had been forced to grow up. All the weight of the business was on my head, and it was forbidden for me to take any money from it to buy myself food if I was hungry. If anything went missing from the market, she withheld my food from me.

Sometimes my aunt would ask if I wanted a beating instead of not eating. I always chose the beating because I needed food from working all day. But most times, I got both with no choice.

Dankey didn't let me play with kids my age. She said, "You don't have time for that any longer."

She took me out of my study class, too. She said, "Because you're out of school, you won't be needing it anymore."

I'm just glad she didn't take me out of church, too. It's the only place I could be without her. The stillness calmed me. I loved how my name was not called out every five seconds. And I was happy I wasn't getting the slap I didn't think I deserved.

At church, I got so lost in the stories it was like I was the only one in the room. This story made me sad, though. It looked like Jesus was troubled by something that was about to happen to him. He told his followers that one of them was going to betray him. As they walked, Jesus went ahead by himself to pray.

He prayed so hard that he looked like he cried blood. I sensed and saw his sadness. I thought about how I felt after my aunt had beaten me for something I didn't do. I wanted to reach out to him but couldn't because we were from two different times.

I never liked when church ended because I had to go home. So, I trudged along. But this particular day, when I got to the house, Beria and uncle were there! My cousin told me why her dad had left the house—because Aunt Dankey kicked him out to sober up. He had stayed with one of his sons. My cousin wanted to see both of her parents, so she asked her dad to come home with her today. I was happy they planned to stay for a few weeks.

Later, Aunt Dankey went to my village and returned with a boy to help with work. He only lasted a week, and she sent him back. I wished it was me going back. He did nothing wrong. She decided she didn't need him, after all. He was about two years older than me and had come from my dad's side of the family.

About a month later, panic broke out in Freetown. Rumors that the rebels were coming to take over the town spread like wildfire. Everyone tried to either escape or hide. My aunt took me, along with her business, to her home village for two months. I had to learn about the little towns around the village because there were no market booths. So, I had to travel from town to town to sell things. I sold more than I ever did back in the city, but some roads were scary—like the road where the truck got stuck on the trip to Freetown. This time I walked across it.

This trip, I became surrounded by deep water and the only thing that kept me from falling in was an old log. But I made it. I was always grateful after crossing safely, especially since I couldn't swim.

On other trips, I wondered if it would be better to cross on a little log or let my aunt do whatever she wanted with me. I wished there was a safer path to these towns—solid paths where I wouldn't fear for my life.

There were several routes like this one, but without logs. But on those, I could get wet to my waist, depending on how deep the water was. Sometimes, leeches attached themselves and sucked my blood. Pulling them off hurt and I bled like crazy. I tried explaining how unsafe these paths were to my aunt. All she said was, "You're just being lazy. I don't want to hear any more of it."

If only this panic would end so we could return to the city, and I wouldn't drown in a river. Every time I crossed one, it reminded me of a story that's been around for generations: A girl is crossing the river. If she stops to talk to any guy, the water will carry her, and she will drown.

Each time, I wondered if I'd recently greeted any guy along the way. I never remembered doing so, but always checked with myself. I hated this story because there was nothing good about it, and the song that leads up to the story is ten times worse.

The moral is obedience. When your parents send you to do something, you don't stop somewhere to do other things. You go straight to the job that was given.

I wished this story wasn't so scary, but that's just African parents for you. Just because of this story, I became afraid of men and boys. Back in the city, a couple of guys cared for me, and I liked them back but couldn't talk to them. They tried hard to talk with me, but I never let them. They bought me food and drinks and I sat six feet away from them—not talking just smiling.

One of them bravely approached me at the market, while my aunt sat there. He tried to talk to me, so I excused myself, saying I needed to use the bathroom. As I ran toward the house, he chased me. I stopped and yelled at him. "I don't want a boyfriend, and I don't like you. If you ever show up again like that, I'll tell my aunt you're trying to steal something."

I hadn't planned to hurt him, just like he hadn't planned to hurt me. Sorry for how I'd made him feel, I wanted to apologize, but I wasn't able to because he moved away. I stayed away from guys that liked me by pretending not to see them. One time, my aunt beat me in front of my friends and some other guys. I had no idea why she did that, but she did. In a way, I was happy the guys that liked me were there to watch. Maybe they'd see I wasn't worth liking, after all.

Indeed, some were ashamed of what they saw, except for one fellow that came over to me, wiped my face, and helped me up from the ground. His name was Bernard and he brought me some cold Kool-Aid from his house and told me about London.

His rich dad owned the house we lived in and more places around Freetown, plus houses in London. His mom stayed in London while his dad went on business trips to Sierra Leone. Sometimes he and his dad stayed for a month or longer. I loved Bernard's stories about London because they made me forget my pain.

One time, my aunt beat me so hard, he became very upset and asked his dad if I could return to London with them. Was he serious? His dad asked me if I really wanted to go with them. I wanted to, but I thought of my parents and declined. What if I wasn't here when my parents came back for me? This boy was the only guy I talked to without fear. They returned to London because of the panic.

I wished there was another town I could go to and sell things without worry for my life. Why was I afraid of dying when my life didn't look that important to my aunt? Was I afraid because I hoped to see my parents again? Maybe I was afraid because no one was there to save me. Or maybe I didn't understand where my fear came from yet.

Rebels

I made a new friend today in the village! She had the same name as me, Isatu. We understood each other so well—she was my mirror image. We spoke the same language, too. I loved her like a sister. We became best friends, stayed up late, played, and told stories.

I spoke to her about the city of Freetown and how I wished she could come with me when we returned. How I longed for her to teach me some new songs. We sang together and joked about being twins. Now, I wanted to stay here longer. But the panic in Freetown had cleared and we would leave in only two weeks. I was sad to part with a loyal friend who I knew I'd never see again.

My heart beat wildly inside. It screamed for protection, but how could I protect myself, when I had no power over my life? I felt like a bird in a cage. With my family, I was free. But now, with my aunt, I felt threatened.

What more could I do? Some days I worried I might never see my family. Why couldn't Dankey take me home to

Moyamba and my family during this panic? Aunt Dankey insisted I never talk or ask about my parents anymore. She actually said I'd never see them again. Those words cut something inside, causing all the blood to drain from me.

At first, I felt nothing. Then my heart bubbled with pain. Before I knew it, tears ran from my eyes. I cried heavily, but without a sound. It hurt so much, I couldn't scream about my pain out loud. I felt pain and rejection. I cried for myself. Why didn't my parents want me? Wasn't I good enough to please my aunt?

Moving back to Freetown felt crazy, like having to start all over again after only two months away. Our rental house remained, but new neighbors with younger children had moved in. I stopped keeping track of the comings and goings of people, since they never stayed long. But my aunt and one other family were stuck like glue in that place.

My aunt continued beating me, and finally; someone informed her that if she didn't stop, she would be kicked out. Since Dankey didn't like being told what to do, she searched for a new place for us.

Years later, the panic was back. But this time, it was different. A group of people who called themselves 'rebels' killed many simple people. They believed the President had too much power. They didn't want to be controlled and told what they could or couldn't do. These rebels planned to take or hurt innocent lives to make their point, so the President would see and give them control. Of course, they should never have power over people or any place in government.

I soon learned these people went mad because of dia-monds. At ten years old, not knowing or understanding the use of diamonds, it made little sense to me that neither the President nor the rebels valued the lives of peaceful people. Both sides manipulated our minds. One day, things were okay. The next, families cried over the death of a loved one.

During this time, no one was allowed to leave the city. The rebel leader told us not to fear. We were safe. We were just to go about our days and do normal things. But it was difficult to sit on the edge of our seats each day and not know what would happen next.

Radios echoed from one house to another and families gathered to listen. Rebel groups grew every day and good people became edgy and scared. It became hard to know who would turn to the rebels. Radios broadcasted bad news of how we had nowhere to go and how devastated this little country would be when the rebels finished with it; it would look red, and voices would cry. They said we would taste the bitterness of war. All hope for my country faded slowly in front of me.

I closed my eyes tight. All I saw was a red sky and flames beneath me. I cried for my country—for all the lives that would soon be taken in ways I didn't even want to imagine.

All of a sudden came **"BOOM, BOOM, BOOM"**—a loud banging on our door!

My body trembled and fear swept over me as I collapsed to the floor. Two men kicked open the door and entered the house, brandishing guns. One man pointed his gun at me and screamed for me to stand. Still shaking, I stood up and felt pee running down my legs as I stared at the gun pointed at me.

They took all of my aunt's merchandise. Another man pointed his gun at her and said they wouldn't kill us today but would be back. They took the entire market and left nothing but our lives, for however long we'd have them. My aunt shook and cried in panic and told Beria and me to pack our clothes. We would move in with Dankey's uncle. Dankey's husband would stay with his oldest son. Beria would join him after we moved.

On the way, streets had cleared of most people. Some were still at the market but appeared troubled, as if they were being forced to sell. These mad people, who wandered through the streets, wanted us to act like everything was fine and normal so they could steal from those with no power to fight back. They had weapons. We had none.

Watching my country suffer made me sick to my stomach. Seeing the hate in the rebel's eyes made my heart cry even more for my country. What would happen to my sweet Sierra Leone? Oh, land that I love. Your children are crying for you. I prayed.

Oh, Jesus, man who walks on water. The one who looks so sweet and fulll of wonders. There's so much I want to know about you. I pray for you to see my country. Please, I don't want my country to turn into blood. I wish you were here so we don't have to die like this.

We were marked. We'd been told we would not die today, but they would come back to kill us. Why did they tell us this when they broke into my aunt's house? Did these rebels talk about whose families they would kill? Did they already hate us long before all this madness? I didn't know these men, but they seemed to know us very well. The fact that they planned our death ate me up inside. Each day I was scared, not knowing if today would be the day—or how I would die.

One week later, a few men showed up where we stayed. One of the people I saw in the group was the boy my aunt brought from Moyamba who she had sent back after a week because she didn't think he was helpful. Maybe he was here to take revenge. This time, the men threatened us and stole all the food in the house. Seeing him with a gun made me sick. I felt betrayed. I asked, "Why did you bring these men to this family and why did you join them?"

He said, "Anyone can join. I joined to protect my family."

I stared at him. "Then, why are they here taking our things?"

He answered, "They planned to kill everyone at this house, but I told them this was my family, so they can't kill us. But, they demanded some food."

So, he did this to save our lives. As they were leaving, he told me no one would kill us. I didn't know if I'd ever see him again. He was two years older than me and there were two other boys in the group that looked like ten-year-olds.

Dankey told me that the rebels were using younger boys now. If they were old enough to carry a gun, they took them from their parents. Sometimes the boys volunteered—to save the family or to save themselves.

She explained that if the boys didn't have any family, to make the boys mean, they would cut them and put some kind of drug, like cocaine, inside them. This would make them do bad things to others with no feelings of guilt or fear.

So many bad things. I didn't want to hear any more horrid things about what the rebels did to people or why they took children from their parents to turn them into killers. Not only that, but apparently, they took girls, too, and used them in other bad ways. It made me sick and scared. I hoped I would never be part of that group of girls.

Each day was full of bad news. Fear was my enemy. With no appetite for food anymore, my aunt worried about me not eating, for the first time. I never thought the day would come when she actually begged me to eat. What was the purpose of eating when you could die any day?

I wasn't alone. My aunt never showed fear but now, even she had little appetite. She lost so much weight. It felt like a gamer somewhere controlled us, with no life or joy. Peace eluded us and we lost all meaning of life. We used to have a reason to wake up every morning and do things, but now we wondered if we would survive another day.

Sometimes, most of us wished it would just happen so it would be over. Waiting was painful and draining. I didn't want to rise, but Dankey insisted I go to the market to sell mangoes. She had no money to buy good things like she used to. The only reason I could sell the fruit was because we had free mango trees around the house.

I walked with fear to the market. What might happen when I got there? It was a long way, too. What would I do if there was a strike? Would I make it back home safely?

I was so worried; I spaced out until a man in a uniform with a gun snapped at me.

"How much for the mangoes?" he shouted.

I shook so much that some fruit fell off the tray. Frightened, I had forgotten how much they cost. I gave him a cheap price, afraid if the price was too high, he would be angry and kill me. I prayed.

Oh, Jesus, why am I so afraid when I know soon there will be no more of my country? This man has so much power.

He looked peaceful as he took a bite of the juicy, sweet mango. A warm smile on his face told me not to worry. He wasn't a bad guy, but how could I tell?

We had soldiers who were supposed to fight for us, but it was hard to tell the difference anymore. Some rebels dressed like our soldiers to fool us. But most of the rebels looked dirty, with scarves tied around their heads and marks down their cheeks. They made themselves look like who they said they were. With a disturbed look in their eyes, they held guns twice as big as themselves.

Despair

For weeks, walking about the marketplace was frightening. Men in uniforms wore guns slung over their shoulders and packs strapped to their backs. Were they here to protect us? Were they the good guys? If so, for how long? We heard most of the good were being killed, some joined the rebels, and some still fought for us. We hoped our soldiers would win, but we couldn't say because so few were left.

Each day, the rebels grew in number. I doubted there would be any chance for civilians to survive this war. Was my country alone? Did anyone else in the world notice what was happening? If so, would they come help us? I felt no one knew, but how could that be? Were we hidden from the rest of the world? "Oh, Mama Salone. Who is coming to save your children? There's no place to hide, nowhere to go. Someone please hear us."

Something inside didn't feel right. I feared that today might be the last time I walked around the market selling anything.

Tired of walking around with mangoes on my head, I found a placed to set them down. People still saw them and I sold a few more. But I couldn't stay. I imagined my aunt would scold me for resting, so I rose and walked around. Minutes later, guns fired. People ran and screamed. "They're coming, they're coming!"

I tried to run, but my feet seemed glued to the ground. In my mind, I shouted, "Someone please help me. I can't move. They're getting closer. Oh, please! They're going to kill me." Tears ran down my face as one rebel got close to my face. His gun bumped me and he took some mangoes from my tray. Then he spat at me. I thought I should tell him how much he owed for the mangoes, but I was silent.

What was I thinking? I should be thankful he didn't kill me. But I still worried about my aunt killing me. Who will get to me first? My aunt or the rebels? Either way, I know I'm wanted by both.

I didn't think she'd believe me, but I headed back to the house to tell Dankey what happened in the market. Of course, after I told her, she said, "You're just being lazy and making excuses. No dinner for you. Go back to the marketplace."

As I was leaving, the same man who took my mangoes came to our house and yelled at us. "We won't allow anyone at the market anymore. No one is buying or selling anything. The streets must be clear. If we see anyone, we will kill them."

I'm glad Aunt Dankey heard this with her own two ears. I wondered how this man knew where I lived. Were they following me? Another rebel who was with him asked me, "Is this your house?"

"No. It belongs to my uncle," I said.

He said, "Don't leave the house."

Another rebel entered, but I didn't know what they were searching for. He turned around and spoke to the others with him. Then they left.

So Dankey changed her mind and allowed me to eat dinner that night. I waited for the beating, but none came, shockingly. She'd never been kind. Usually if she gave me food, she beat me instead. Was she tired tonight? Maybe she didn't think it was worth it, since we could die soon. For the first time, I saw love in her eyes. She drew me close and said, "You are so special to me. I love you so much."

I said, "I love you too." But I didn't think she believed me. After all, I always wanted to run away from her and go home to my family. I had loved and respected her through fear. But that day, I loved her very much. Maybe it was the fear I saw in her now: the fear of death.

Even though she was concerned more for her life than my own, I didn't want her to die, and I truly hoped she would make it out alive. Hopefully, one of many who might survive. Would my family be among them? I hadn't heard from them for a long time. The last time I saw them, I had my older sister, Fatmata, my brother, Ali, a one-year-old sister, and mom was expecting another baby. Were they alive or dead?

A few days later, we received word that the rebels would come from the surrounding villages. They named some of the destroyed villages and Moyamba was one. After I heard that, my hope for my family with small children faded. I only hoped Dad had found a safe place for them to hide.

As the night drew near, fresh foreboding kicked in. I couldn't sleep for fear the rebels would kill us during the night while we slept. So I stayed up late and thought of things to calm myself. I imagined I told stories with my friends. I thought about the fun games we played at school and my teacher's kind smiles. I remembered my Sunday School teacher and all the wonderful stories he'd shared. There was so much more to learn. Oh, how I wished I knew all about Jesus. Now I might never have the chance.

I remembered all the boys that had liked me, but I'd never liked back and wished I had been nicer to them. When my aunt and I moved to the village to hide from the first panic, I met Isatu, who became my best friend. Was she still alive? What about my uncle and my cousin Beria? My mind filled with thoughts, but my eyes grew heavy and finally closed for some time.

BOOM!

A loud bomb-like noise startled me. Everyone in the house woke and I heard crying. Smoke rose from different directions. Someone in the house said, "The war is here!"

We had nowhere to go. It was the end of Salone. Still dark at two o'clock in the morning, everyone panicked as they rounded up their kids and families. Some people just ran around aimlessly. A second bomb exploded. Was the first one just to wake us up? The second meant it was time for their one-sided war. The rebels would win, for they outnumbered our soldiers.

At five o'clock, it was still dark and gloomy, as if the sun was afraid to rise like most of us. The clouds were gray and heavy, but no rain came. The sun peeked out and went back to hide behind the clouds. Oh, if only we could do the same! Stillness held us for a moment, and now everyone was afraid to make a sound. It was hard for mothers with small children and babies. Some tried nursing their babies just to stop them from making any type of noise.

More bombs went off, followed by gunshots. People ran. Some of them suffered wounds, while others sought cover. My uncle's house was now packed with people with nowhere to run. We sat as if we were in timeout; waiting to be slaughtered. One man ran toward our house, covered in blood, and said, "They're coming, they're coming!"

I ran inside to hide under the bed, but there was no space. That was fine, as they would probably look there first. I went outside, tied a scarf around my head, and rubbed white clay dirt over my face so they'd think I was sick and leave me alone. Other girls in the house did the same.

Our neighbors came over to sit with us. No one said much, but as we sat close together, our eyes filled with tears. What could we say we'd remember after we were dead and gone? All we could do now was sit, wait, and hope all this would pass us. Maybe the rebels would change their minds and stop the war.

Then my aunt asked me to bring her a drink. As I stood up, someone behind me told me to sit down. I turned and saw a man covered with guns and five more men with him. Some carried machetes and axes. My stomach dropped, and I felt like I had to pee, but I had none to do so.

The leader came and looked the younger kids over and over. He picked three girls and three boys including me. They lined us up to go with them. No one spoke or came to our rescue, for everyone was consumed by fear as we left.

Knowing my work with her was done, I tearfully looked at my aunt one last time. I might never see her again.

Terror

I trudged along to cause a delay to wherever we were going. One man shoved me with the end of his gun to make me move faster. He threatened to shoot me if I didn't speed up.

If I obeyed, would they have mercy on us? Though I didn't know where they were taking us, I was sure that each step led to my death.

Oh Jesus, I don't know you that well, but in your book it shows how great you are: how you calmed the seas that were about to drown your disciples and how you healed the sick with just words. I don't know how to pray or know if you can hear me, but I hope you can. I pray you can save us like you did your disciples. Please don't let these men kill us and please don't let them win this war.

I looked up at one man and asked, "What will you do to us?"

Without hesitation, his eyes held mine and said, "We're going to kill you all."

At that, emptiness swallowed any remaining hope. There was no way out now; the look on his face showed it. Inside I cried. *Please don't let them kill us. Please, Jesus, I don't want to die like this. Please don't let them. Please, I pray.* They took us to Black Tank, the water tank for the area, and lined us up against the wall of a house that sat about five houses away.

One man shouted. "If any of you try to run, we will chop you in half."

I sobbed and moaned. No longer could I hold my tears back. I wanted to run, but couldn't. I didn't want to be in either the front or the back of the line. Why would that matter? Was I going crazy? Someone started a ring of fire around us to keep us from escaping.

One said, "Now you will taste the bitterness of war."

I wailed. *What does that mean?* Then one man pulled out an axe and called to one of the neighbor boys to come over and lay down on their stomach, which he did. The rebel raised the axe and brought it down swiftly. My eyes squinted shut: I was afraid to watch. When I opened them, the boy's hands were cut off.

"This is the bitterness of war. We're cutting all your hands off so you can go tell your president," one of them said.

Two more went before me. I couldn't watch. My heart beat faster and faster. Their cries told how painful it was. Then it was my turn. I laid on my stomach and they cut my right hand off first, then the left. So much pain! Was my heart cut out? I couldn't stand. My body went numb for a few seconds. When I finally stood, my hands still hung from thin pieces of skin. Blood sprayed all around, and then the world went dark. People screamed and cried, but I saw nothing. I blacked out for some time.

When I awoke, I struggled back home, but no one was around. From the back of the house, people ran in every direction. Fire blazed from the neighbor's house. People were still inside! One man was burning as he left that house. He cried, "Someone help me!" His eyes, filled with pain, met mine. I cried harder now, because I was sorry I wasn't able to help.

Weakness caused the world to spin around me. Dizzy, I searched for my aunt, but she was gone. Not sure of where to go or what to do, I stumbled across the man who had been on fire. His wife laid dead on the ground, too. "Oh, no. Jesus," I cried.

Everyone I knew was dying. My heart was dying, too. Blood continued to spray from my body. I didn't want to see any more death. I tried to run but couldn't. So, I found refuge under some banana plants. Too weak to walk any more, I sat and hid from everything.

My hands grew heavy, hanging from me like they were. With so much blood lost, I thirsted. And I wanted to use the bathroom, but no one was around to help me.

Gunfire continued in every direction. Bombs exploded every second. Finally, the crying and screaming stopped. What was that? Was everyone dead but me? How much longer would *I* have? I didn't think I'd see the morning. I'd die alone with no family near.

This hurt so much! How I needed Mom to hold me before I died. I missed her desperately. I longed for her to tell me stories of when I was a baby and how much she wanted me. Oh, if she could sing to me so my pain would disappear.

Frightened, I wondered why I had to die like this. What did I do wrong? Why did I feel I was marked for this? If I survived, what good would I be to Dankey? I was nothing but a pair of hands to her. Now, I'm less than nothing.

Tears streamed down my face, which burned from all the crying. All hope gone, I gave up and waited for death, but some force kept me from it. I begged it to let go because I saw nothing after this.

As I sat crying, a still voice inside told me everything would be alright. I tried to fight that voice with the facts as I knew them. A warm peace settled over me. A loving presence held me, a feeling I'd never felt before. Someone loved me I couldn't see. Oh, how much I wanted to see who loves me so. Unlike my parents' love, it was more—and different. I cried still, but for a new reason: someone I could not see loved me. No longer was I afraid of death or anything else. Something inside me changed.

My fingers swelled up—all life gone from them. My hands hung on with an increasing heaviness. I wished they'd just fall off. Blood ran out as if it would never stop. I let my head fall and tried to sleep. Then, footsteps!

A guy with a gash on his back ran toward me. I hoped he had escaped death. With sorrow, he asked, "Do you need help?"

"Could you bring me some water?" I asked. He jumped over the fence. Had I frightened him? No, he came back with water for me. It was hard to drink though, because blood kept getting into it, but I swallowed a few drops. I would be forever grateful for this man's kindness.

After a while, more people came to share my hiding spot. Small as it was, strangers soon crowded the place. An older man said, "You can't stay here forever, you realize. You must look for your family or someone else. If you like, you can come with us when we leave, and we'll help you find them."

Should I stay in case anyone I knew returned, or is everyone dead? I knew I couldn't stay here alone again another night, so I followed them. We saw many dead bodies covered with flies. It made me sick to my stomach.

I thought about turning around, but I wanted to find my aunt. Maybe if I closed my eyes, I wouldn't have to see death. I cried again when I saw kids, even younger than me, on the ground, dead. One mother lay dead with her baby on her back. Was the child shot with his or her mother? Or did they die from suffocation from being tied to her back? One lady in the group asked, "Would you like to cover your eyes with my headscarf so you don't have to see this?"

I thought about that for a while and said, "What if we come across some rebels and have to run? How will I know what to do? Will you leave me and protect yourself?"

Her eyes caught mine, and she said, "I will keep you safe as long as I can, so please trust me."

So, I did. We finally passed all the dead people in sight. She untied the scarf, and we walked some more. My steps are slowing as I became weakened and lightheaded, so I stopped to catch my breath.

A group of rebels traveling on another path saw us. They pointed their guns and screamed, "Don't move! Hands up!"

Again, my heart sank, and I fell hard on the ground. I was out. When I woke up, I had so much pain from the fall. Some people that had been with me now lay dead. I rose quickly and sought the lady that had loaned me her scarf, but she was gone. Alone, I knew of nowhere to go or what to do, so I hid behind someone's house.

I couldn't stay because rebels marched up and down in search of more people to kill. Would anyone be home? I needed to use the bathroom and hoped someone would help me with my pants. The house had no door and everything inside was gone. The rebels had already been there. They'd written on the outside and inside walls the word "RUF" which was what they called themselves. Exhausted, I entered the house and laid down on the floor. I couldn't stop the pee from coming and apologized. "I'm sorry I couldn't pull my pants down." I fell asleep.

Separated

When I woke the next day, it was Friday. Remembering the days of the week made me feel smart. I forgot for a while that we were in a war and that my hands were cut off. Had it all been a dream? The pain reminded me it wasn't. I tried lifting my hands, but my blood had glued them to the cement floor. The harder I tried, the more it hurt. I laid on my stomach, unable to move much, not knowing if I'd ever be free from this position.

Some man walked toward the house, and I called out to him for help. He just looked at me and walked away. I repeated my plea louder. "Please don't leave me like this." He never came back. Sadly, I recognized this man as a friend of my aunt's who I used to take food to. Now he walked away like he never knew me. I laid my head down, hope gone, and waited to die.

Something inside me fought for life. For what? I was a nobody. No one wanted me. My aunt wasn't looking for me. And even though I tried to find her, I realized that if I found her, she probably would walk away from me or finally take me back to my parents—if she found them. I would be useless to her.

At least my blood stopped running down my arm. Maybe I was out of blood. I moved little by little until both of my hands were free from the ground. I had hoped the skin connected to my hands would fall away, but it didn't. Were my hands heavier today, or was I just weaker?

Outside, the world was silent. No cars honked, no people screamed over each other to sell their goods, no school bells rang, no dogs barked, no parents yelled at their children, no children cried or laughed. A country, once filled with happiness and joy, now laid in desolate grief.

For a split second, I forgot where I was. I used to fetch water here, but the rebels burnt most buildings. Where was I going? Who was I looking for? I doubted my aunt was alive to find.

In the stillness, I wondered if the war was over and how many people remained alive.

Did the rebels go back to wherever they came from? Are they happy now that they'd destroyed everything and everyone? Are they sorry for destroying their country, for the innocent blood which soaked into the soil, or the nursing babies who lay dead with their mothers who never knew the meaning of the war?

How could anyone do this? They even shot the dogs dead. Nauseous, for once I was thankful my stomach had nothing to lose.

I sought someone who might help me and came to the house of a kind young lady who wasn't hurt. My arms ached more because of the burden of the extra weight of my dead hands. She took one look and removed a wrap she wore around her waist. She tied it around my neck and made a sling for my hands.

I smiled, thankful for the relief from the weight and for finding this gracious lady and her family. I hoped my presence wouldn't bring harm to them. Sometimes, shooting pain in my arns left me crying. I didn't want the rebels to find this family because of my cries.

People still hid, so I didn't think the war was over yet. To spare them, I told her I needed to find my family, which didn't please the lady. But I told her I must go and thanked her for her kindness.

As I left, footsteps came from the back of the house, so I quickly hid in the bathroom. Had they seen me go in? Someone pounded on the door and called out, "Come on out!" Just as I was about to come out, they ran and shouted after someone else down the street. I didn't understand what that was, but I believed something saved me.

As I walked down the street, a guy in uniform called out to me. "Who did this to you?"

What would he do to me if I told him? I said nothing, so he asked again with a demanding voice. I said, "It was someone like you."

He said, "No. Soldiers don't kill or hurt innocent people. My job is to find people and put an end to this terror."

I hoped there was more of him because one soldier couldn't stop all the rebels. I turned to walk away.

He called out again. "Can you walk?"

"I'm tired." I didn't know what he was thinking.

A man ran out like he was being chased, and this soldier called out to him to stop. He did, but he ran again when the soldier yelled, "Stop or I'll shoot you. I need you to carry this little girl for me. She can't walk. I'll tell you where to go."

What in the world? Why would he threaten someone's life for me? And where would he take me? The man lifted me over his shoulder, but hanging over this man's back was worse than walking. He shook terribly and my arms bumped his back, renewing the pain. "Where are you taking me?" I asked.

The soldier answered. "To someone who can help you."

To the man being forced to carry me, I said, "I'm sorry."

He said, "That's okay. I don't mind helping you. I was afraid because I thought I was going to be shot. You can't trust anyone."

By this point, I didn't figure I had much to worry about. Eventually, my blood would all drain out of me and I would be dead and gone. "You can put me down."

He did this, but the soldier yelled at me. "Get back on this man."

"I'd rather walk," I said.

The soldier said, "I'm trying to help you, not watch you die. The place we're going isn't far now."

When we arrived at a big house with a gate, he knocked on the door until a man opened it. "There's no more room," he said.

The soldier said, "You need to make room for this girl." Then the soldier and the man who'd carried me left.

The troubled man allowed me to join them. There wasn't much room to walk around, as there were so many wounded people—all in so much pain. Blood and cuts covered many of them. Other's eyes revealed the pain of loss of someone close to them.

This man who opened the door was risking his life to help all these people, and now I was among them. What if my pain worsened and the rebels found us and killed everyone because of me? I didn't want to stay. I said, "I want to go look for my aunt." This would help him get me out before I brought more grief.

"What is your aunt's name?" he asked.

"Dankey," I said.

He told someone to ask around for Dankey and excused himself. He returned with some food for me to eat. After he left, someone said they'd found my aunt! Excited by the news that she was alive, when I approached her, she didn't look like she missed me or cared at all about what had happened to me. Why didn't she even ask where I'd been all this time, or how I'd found her? Nothing had changed. She was her old self, just trying to survive the war. I asked her, "How did you find this place? Were you hurt?"

Dankey said, "No, but I brought one of the girls that got her hands cut off with you."

"Why didn't you look for me?" I asked.

"Because I thought you were dead."

I guessed that made sense.

Minutes later, the owner introduced himself to me as a doctor. He inspected my hands. "I'm not able to reattach them because there's only a little piece of skin holding them. The only option is to cut them off. I'm sorry I have nothing to numb the pain. It will hurt a little."

"Oh, please, no more pain," I sobbed.

He said, "We have to cut them off so I can treat your arms better. If we don't, you will likely get sick and die."

"Alright," I said. I agreed, not because I was afraid to die, but because I didn't want to carry their weight anymore.

I followed him. My aunt didn't want to come along, but she did because someone forced her. The pain was too much. It didn't hurt a little—it hurt a lot. Someone gave me something to bite on so I didn't scream. Finally it was over, but the pain wasn't. The doctor cleaned and wrapped my wounds. It felt good not to have my hands pulling me down, but I missed them. They were part of me. Then they weren't. Part of me was dead and part was not.

I regarded my dead hands and thought of all the difficult things they had been through: blisters from making raw soaps, cuts from household chores, getting whipped on them, and more. Why were they taken from me? What had they done wrong?

The doctor asked, "Do you want me to bury them?"

"What?" I asked. I didn't know I had that choice. Wouldn't he just throw them away?

He said, "Some people save them to show them to the rebel leaders while others bury them. If you like, I will bury them for you, so one day, when you go to heaven, your hands will be there waiting for you."

That sounded much better to me than showing them to a rebel leader.

Heaven sounded like a beautiful place. I remembered my Sunday school teacher told the class that he would talk about heaven where the Messiah Jesus came from the next time we met. I had little hope for that class now.

Does Jesus look the way I imagined him from the stories? So perfect and kind, he looks nothing like us. He heals so many and has a love for everyone. If only he was here to heal all those who hurt and fill our poor hearts with love. Heaven is lucky to have Jesus.

Here, all we had were people who mutilated and killed each other for nothing. How would I reach heaven? I didn't even know where it was. All I knew was my country.

How my hands would get to heaven was another question with no answer. I wished I could believe my hands would wait for me in heaven, but I couldn't. My head ached and I couldn't think any more, even though the headache distracted me from the pain in my arms. The doctor brought me some medicine to relieve the pain, since I cried from it. I hated crying because people looked at me as if it would get everyone killed. Some even looked like they'd throw me out if they could.

Hospital

Just before darkness fell, the gates opened. The soldier that had brought me earlier now brought men to guard the gate, food, and supplies. He checked on me to see how I was doing. He told me he'd send trucks in the morning to take all of us to the hospital.

Part of me didn't want him to leave. I hadn't felt love like this since I was in Moyamba with my family: the way Dad loved me. The way this man cared for me reminded me of Dad. When he left, I worried. I hoped for the best for him and that he would return safely.

In the morning, everyone waited and waited for the promised trucks. An hour passed and people wondered if the worst had happened because sometimes those who had shown kindness before, had gotten hurt or died. Would a truck come? Why did these people get hurt, but my aunt didn't? I squelched tears, because I believed I had lost another friend, and laid down, hoping to sleep until the next day. Tears fell anyway.

But a few minutes later, someone opened the gate. Two men arrived and told everyone to get into the trucks: those without hands or legs first. The doctor told me to follow him and that my aunt would ride in a different truck. He led me to my soldier friend.

Oh, I was happy to see him alive! Maybe not everyone that loved me had to die, after all. He was the driver, and he set me in the back with the others. He left no one behind.

The first truck with soldiers led the way—guns at the ready. Three trucks with civilians followed. A fifth truck of soldiers with guns, a few civilians, and me, brought up the rear. The soldiers would fire at anyone who tried to stop us from reaching the hospital.

Would we make it? Anxious, I worried because we had to stop at checkpoints and allow a search of each truck for suspicious activity. The soldiers we saw along this road were different. They wore blue helmets with the letter UN on them. Once, one climbed into our truck. He looked at me and spoke in an unfamiliar language to one of our soldiers. This soldier told me not to be afraid. He would ride with us to the hospital so we wouldn't have to be stopped anymore. Another blue-helmet soldier rode in the front truck, too.

The trip was gruesome. All around us, dead people laid. A graveyard had more people, but they were buried, so I couldn't see them. But these poor victims I saw—and smelled. I wished I didn't have to see this and closed my eyes, but I saw them, even then. I tried to keep my head down so I wouldn't see any more.

But someone screamed. I lifted my head and saw a man being dragged to a wall. I dropped my head fast. A gunshot rang out. A soldier in the truck said, "We finally caught all these bastards. They're getting what they deserve."

My friend, the driver, came back and sat by me for a minute. "The war is almost over," he said. "UN men are here to help with that and more are coming. They've surrounded the hospital to protect it. Don't be afraid any longer. You're going to be safe."

The closer we got to the city's center, the more UN people I saw and a lot more dead bodies. This time, the dead were not just civilians, but rebels as well. They captured some rebels, but many refused to surrender and died fighting. The rebels had tried to enter the hospital to kill the doctors and everyone else. They hated that other countries had come to stop them and all the mess they'd made, especially the UN. But the UN soldiers appeared to be winning.

We arrived at the hospital, which was guarded by a lot of security, like my friend had said. Now I felt safer. Surprisingly, people sold cooked food, like fish and bread, rice and stew, and cakes and cookies. I hadn't eaten in two days and the food made me hungry. Many people pretended to be hurt as they tried to find protection inside the hospital, but they allowed only those actually needing treatment.

My friend helped me out of the truck and sat me on a bench by my aunt inside the hospital to wait for a doctor. He gave Dankey some money and said goodbye. I wanted to beg him to stay, but something inside me told me not to be selfish. He needed to help more people like me.

Tears welled up as I watched him leave. Aunt Dankey got upset with me for acting weird about a guy I didn't even know. Well, she's right. I knew little about him except for his caring. I hoped someone would show him kindness in return. I wiped my face on my shoulders and acted like I was fine, because my aunt hated for me to show signs of weakness.

Once I caught the measles and felt terrible. It gave me chills, and I was so weak that even walking around hurt. Had there been a treatment for measles? If so, she wouldn't have given it to me because she gave me nothing—not even her sympathy. All I got from her was yelling about how lazy I was being. Bumps had covered my skin, so I rubbed white clay all over to help it dry and heal faster. I had sat outside under the sun and waited for the clay to dry—the sun had been my medicine. It warmed me and I had ended up falling asleep on the floor.

But Dankey didn't care, like always. If some kids beat me up and I came home with blood on my forehead, she'd never ask or care unless I fought back. Those kids told their parents and then I'd be in trouble with everyone. It never mattered how I was treated or if I got sick. So I kept everything to myself and acted like she could never hurt me or break me. But I knew that was a lie.

As we waited in the hospital, I became lightheaded. The next thing I knew, I was in a room on a bed hooked up to various medical things. They'd wrapped my arms in clean bandages. I had many questions. "What happened? How did I get into this room?"

Dankey answered. "You passed out, Mariatu."

I wondered how many more times I could pass out. I continued. "Who is Mariatu?"

She said, "That's your name now."

My parents named me Isatu. Where did Dankey come up with the name Mariatu, and what gave her the right to change the name my parents gave me? She probably thought I had forgotten everything, but I hadn't. I may not have known how I got into this room, but I remembered who I was. "What are all these things hanging on me?"

The doctor answered. "These keep you alive. You needed fluid and blood because you've lost a lot. This will be your room until you're well enough to go home. I'll see you every day and make sure you're recovering. You'll have a nurse that will help you, too, with things like washing, dressing, and even feeding."

He left, and a nurse brought in a big bowl of rice and stew. Aunt Dankey put some in a little bowl and fed me. She complained the whole time. Eating wasn't fun anymore, and I cried because she made me feel guilty about what happened to me. She said, "I hate having to be here with you. Don't get used to me feeding you or anything else when you're healed. You'll have to learn how to take care of yourself because we're going back to doing the market."

I wanted to die, so I didn't have to live under her again. Being like this would be ten times worse than before.

Thankfully, my nurse walked in and asked if I was ready to be washed. I was self-conscious about the marks on my body from beatings, but she asked no questions and washed me quickly. I held my arms up high to keep the stubs from getting wet, which was uncomfortable, but I managed.

Afterward, I felt like a new person: clean and smelling good. I wanted to forget the war, but couldn't in this place where I saw people with all sorts of problems: missing ears, legs, and even injured babies. How could anyone do evil to a baby? Mothers sat by their children and helped them, but my aunt sat in my room—distant. What was she thinking?

Sad for her, I knew she hadn't heard a word about her daughter or husband, not that she cared much about him. I hoped they were alive and well, so she might find her daughter again.

At night, it was hard to sleep. Gunshots sounded outside the hospital and screams followed. Covering my ears didn't help, and neither did the pain pulsing in my arms.

My nurse brought me medicine to ease the pain and said, "You should be able to fall asleep soon so you don't have to hear all the shooting. The rebels are trying to come inside the building by acting like civilians, so many of them are being killed."

I wondered if they were killing the wrong people. What if they were really civilians trying to get help? I wished all the killing would stop. I hoped for peace and laughter, even though that would take some time. But I hoped that someday, we would laugh, play, and trust again.

Healing

I closed my eyes and dreamed I was five again in Moyamba. My sister, Fatmata, chased me and I ran as fast as my little feet could take me; through the peanut field and straight through the swampy rice field. She wasn't running at her fastest because she didn't catch me until we reached our house. Mom and Dad laughed when they saw how breathless she was and she laughed, too. Dad put me on his shoulders so I could pick an orange from a tree. As I struggled to pull the orange free, someone called my name. "Hold on, I'm coming," I said.

A cool hand brushed my face. I opened my eyes and saw the nurse standing by the bed. My eyes closed again so I could finish the dream, but that didn't work. I wished I had enough time to finish my dream about my family. "Rise and shine," the nurse said. "It's time to clean your arms and after that, you can eat."

That sounded like a trap, and food would be my reward. They took me into a room with a tub filled with water, which rolled like it was boiling, but no steam came off it. I'd never seen anything like it before, and I was told to put my arms in it. I fled the room, but had nowhere to run.

They brought me back and closed the door behind me, so I couldn't escape. Oh, well. I gave up. What was the point of fighting things I couldn't control? Their faces didn't appear mean. They were there to help, not hurt me. I did as I was told and put my arms into the bubbling water, one at a time, to clean them.

I found the experience ugly and excruciatingly painful—far worse than when they were severed! My favorite part was when they wrapped up my arms, because that meant the agony would stop. This I had to endure every day until they healed enough.

I was thankful the hospital took good care of me, even if it wasn't the way I had hoped for. It was encouraging to watch the doctors and nurses helping others with care. What would my life be like after discharge?

Weeks later, Aunt Dankey said, "I'm going to send for your family to come for you, if they're still alive."

"What if they're not?" I asked. She didn't respond. I hoped she could find them so I wouldn't be homeless.

"I'm going to find Beria and build a little market she can handle herself," she said.

I wished her well with everything.

If only this war had never happened. Even though I had always wanted to be free from her, it made me a little sad that we would be parted now. I didn't want it to happen like this. War had damaged more inside than outside. Outside wounds healed, but healing the inside would be difficult for most of us. Nightmares of war made me sick, like I re-lived it over and again. I wished I could leave these bad dreams behind.

After two months in the hospital, my arms were healing and they didn't hurt anymore when I plunged them into the big tub of water. I walked around the hospital compound and made some friends my age. Some had one hand cut off. Others got their hands or arms beat up with machetes. These experiences were not great topics of conversation, but we also shared where we'd come from and hoped we'd see each other again outside the hospital.

Every once in a while, the hospital sent guys to visit the patients. They traveled from room to room and we didn't always see the same men. Some asked about the war and what we thought of the people that hurt us and whether we remembered them. It made me uncomfortable to talk about it. Did they want me to identify them so they could find them? I remembered some of them, but I wouldn't look for them—or help these men seek revenge.

The damage was done, and I had to go on with what I had. I should be grateful to be living, because many others didn't make it. These visitors asked too many unwanted questions, like they might have taken revenge on the rebels if I told them who they were.

I enjoyed the days when I had visitors who brought books to read to me. I couldn't read, so hearing the stories made me want to learn. Every time they read, I jumped into the stories to be part of it. I saw the characters move and understood why they made the choices they did. It was a pleasure to have people visit, because the hospital could be depressing, with little to do.

My arms were healing, but I needed to have the bones in both arms shaved because they stuck out and caused me some pain. Ready to go to the surgery waiting room, Aunt Dankey told me to go alone, because she didn't think they would allow her there.

People waiting for operations packed the area. I didn't mind the wait, as I had nowhere to go, but I was anxious about feeling more pain. The patients were nervous; their faces looked like they were expecting to be shot. Maybe if I left and missed my turn, they would reschedule me for another day, when I might feel better, so I returned to my room.

Not long after I left, someone knocked on my door. An unfamiliar nurse said, "Come with me. The doctors are waiting to operate on your arms."

"Doctors?" It must be serious if it took more than one person to do this. I walked into the room and felt sick. Were the chances of dying higher than coming out alive? I had to remove all my clothes. What kind of place was this? I had never been in this kind of situation. Scared, I even asked, "May my aunt come in and watch over me?"

"No. We only allow the doctors and nurses in here," the nurse said.

I had never once seen a doctor before the war and didn't understand how things ran in the hospital. I wished I knew. My heart beat so fast and hard, I thought it might jump out of my chest. I panicked about being naked around strangers. I could die before my surgery unless my heart calmed down. A nurse handed me a gown to put on and then walked me into a room with lots of strange, fancy things I didn't understand.

"Lay on this bed," one of them said.

I laid on this narrow bed-looking table. Above it was a big, round light with different colors inside. The doctors asked me something, but I kept staring at the light and was getting tired. The last thing I remembered was the doctor asking me a question: "What is your age?"

Back in my room, I laid in bed with things hanging over me again. I felt intense pain in my arms, as if someone had severed my hands again. Thankfully, my nurse kept bringing me pain medicine whenever I needed it.

After about a week, my arms were doing much better, except I woke up with tiny bumps covering my body. Where did they come from? They itched like crazy. The nurse gave me something for the itching, bathed me, and rubbed some kind of cream on me, which I had to let dry before I dressed. The next day, the bumps had dried up and itched less.

They would discharge me in two weeks. I was happy I could search for my family, but I was also sad. If I couldn't find them, no one would take care of me, like my nurse. Aunt Dankey already told me she didn't want me.

The gunfire outside had stopped for weeks now. Patients from the hospital could go outside and return with food. I was one of the few who hadn't been outside since I arrived. I was okay with that. Those people were brave to do such a thing. I feared stepping foot outside the hospital: still afraid of being attacked or killed. I watched them and saw no fear in their faces. They wanted to live their lives without fear, or maybe they just knew how to hide it.

But I was transparent and still jumpy. One day, an older man ran around screaming in the hospital compound. What did I do? Ran to my room and hid under the bed. The hospital had already discharged most of the kids I met. I wasn't able to say goodbye to them. I was one of the younger children and one of the last to be discharged, because I was also one of the last to arrive.

Those final two weeks flew by. All the other kids were gone, so I was happy to leave. I would miss the security of the hospital. No more protection. Back to life in the outside world filled with many people. Since I brought nothing with me to the hospital, I had little to carry: only the two gowns they gave me.

The doctor and nurse came to see me. My arms had completely healed now. They removed my stitches the week before and everything looked good. My nurse hugged me, as did my doctor. They both walked my aunt and me to the hospital gate, where a taxi waited for us.

Family

I held in tears. I would miss the love and kindness of the doctors and nurses. Dankey instructed the taxi driver on how to find her uncle's house. Would the house be standing? Would anyone be home? On the way, I saw some people selling and walking, but the streets were not as crowded as before. It made me sad to see wounded people begging for food and more. I hoped that wouldn't be me when my aunt threw me out. I hoped she would find my parents.

The driver rolled down his window, and the warm summer breeze blew across my face. Lovely! It reminded me of when Dad took me with him to work one day. The sun shone and a warm breeze blew over the rice field, which released a delicious fragrance into the air. With every breath, I had taken this fresh air into my lungs. How incredible that day had been!

Today was like that, but without the yummy scent. The sun still baked the blood left in some places, which stank. The driver rolled up his window, for which I was thankful.

Could he read my mind? I loved feeling the breeze and the warmth of the sun—just not the smell of death.

The driver pulled up to the house: the place where my terror had started. My heartbeat rose, and I replayed the events of that day over and over in my mind. I closed my eyes tight to stop seeing them, but that didn't work. Crying, I said, "I don't want to go. I don't want to go."

Aunt Dankey, who had no sympathy, told the driver, "Take her back to the hospital."

But the driver understood and had compassion. "You may stay in the car until you're ready to come out. The war is over now and no one will hurt you again. The people who did this to you are probably dead."

I listened, but still stared at the house and wished for people to come out: people I knew were dead. I hoped I would see the guy who was on fire or his wife who died in front of me. Of course, I wouldn't. Now Aunt Dankey held their three sobbing children in her arms. I couldn't help but cry, too, for their loss. My cousin Beria walked toward the taxi and the driver let me out to meet her. Oh, I was happy to see her alive and well. Seeing her gave me hope, although I didn't understand why.

The war had hardened people, so they lacked trust. Some looked angry or depressed. Myself, I didn't think I'd be useful without hands. Embarrassed, I hid them behind my clothes so people wouldn't stare at me. In the hospital, it was better because everyone related to me, and I them. There, hiding wasn't necessary. Some days, I hid behind the house alone and let the sun soak into my skin while I slept for about an hour. My aunt never cared what I did anymore.

I'd lost weight since my hospital stay because of the lack of care. Some days, I didn't eat until the evening, or whenever Aunt Dankey felt like giving food to me. I disgusted her, and she found someone else to help me.

Often, I wanted to run away and never come back. Maybe I should look for my family myself. If only I knew where they were, things might be different. But what if they were ashamed of me, like my aunt? Oh, I hoped that wouldn't be the case. My heart couldn't handle much more pain.

Even though everyone said the war was over, I felt like it wasn't. I feared it might start all over again. Every night I saw the war in my sleep. Sometimes in my dreams, I tried to hide from the rebels to avoid capture. If I wasn't able to escape, I'd end up shot in the chest, struggling to breathe.

That woke me up, and I stayed awake, so I didn't go back into that nightmare. I laid on my back and tried to think of beautiful thoughts, but none came to mind. I listened to the bird's songs in the morning. Oh, how I wished I could be one of them: flying, walking, singing, and going wherever I liked.

The sun rose early, so I walked to the mountain close to the house. If I could climb high enough, I might feel like I could fly. If I fell, I would learn how to stand up. I needed to learn how to care for myself, but didn't know how, yet. At least I thought about it.

The sun was extra-kind today. Even my shaved head loved it. Yes, my aunt shaved my head. She thought it would be better for me and she wouldn't have to do my hair. I didn't argue. I'd rather have a shaved head that her hurting my head every time she tried to brush it.

On my way home, a man who resembled my dad stood under a mango tree and watched me. Unsure if he was Dad, I put my head down. Then he called to me. "Isatu!"

My *real* name. I lifted my head and realized he *was* my dad! We both cried as he ran to pick me up in his arms. I wrapped my arms around his neck. "Oh, me papa, me papa. Please take me home. I want to see Mom."

When we arrived at my aunt's house, dad realized Dankey hadn't taken good care of me. His face grew so angry, I thought he might hit her. I was glad he didn't. I told him it wasn't her fault; it was the war. He took what few things I had, and we left. No matter what she had done to me, or how she made me feel, I still loved and respected her. I knew she had love within her. She just didn't know how to show it.

I loved every minute with my dad. Was this a dream? "Pinch me, Dad. Show me you're real." He laughed, but pinched me anyway. It felt real to me and I guessed it wasn't a dream. We reached the place where my parents stayed: a marketplace where people used to sell food and things. Now, because of the war, the homeless camped here without roofs over their heads or food to eat.

The rest of the family cried when they saw me. I hated all the crying and wanted it to stop, but Mom couldn't stop. "The rebels captured Fatmata during the war. They've released some of the other girls, but not your sister. I don't know if she's still alive."

My heart hurt for Mom at this news. "Don't feel sorry for me. I know my sister will come home and we'll all live together and be happy again."

Mom's eyes held mine as she said, "You don't have to be strong. You have every right to be sad and angry."

I agreed with her, but I chose not to be sad or angry because I had my family with me now and, one day, my sister would return to us.

The marketplace was home to those without one. It was sad to see my family living like this. They used to have so much, but now, we barely had anything to eat for the day. Every day, hopeful people moved in, adding to the thousands already there. People got sick or died from lack of food and poor living conditions.

Some planned to stay and built makeshift houses, like tents, with palm branches for roofing. Dad built one for our family, but it was too small for all of us to sleep in. There were six children now, including me, plus Mom, Dad, mom's mom, and my grandma.

We squeezed inside and just fit on rainy days, but when the weather was nice, the kids slept outside by the tent. And most times, Grandma insisted she sleep outside so I could sleep with my parents. I rejected her idea and slept with her outside. I loved Grandma very much and remembered how she spoiled me back in Moyamba. She used to pack my bag to see her every time I got angry with my parents. She had lived only five blocks away, but to me, it felt like another village.

When Aunt Dankey took me from Moyamba, I thought I'd never see Grandma again, but here I was, sitting by my favorite person in the world, who still spoiled me. Since I returned, she saw that I had warm water to bathe in. She made sure I was always warm when it was cold outside and made tea for me so I wouldn't catch a cold. She scratched my back, sang to me, told me stories of when I was a baby and how I was born in the shower. If it wasn't for her then, I would have hit the ground, but she caught me just in time.

We had a strong connection. I never had to ask for her help; she knew what I wanted before I asked. The days we had food to eat, she hid hers away and gave it to me later, if I was hungry. I was lucky to have a grandmother like her, and I was happy she was here.

The Hut

For a month, we lived in the camp. News circulated about the rebels hiding outside the city releasing some girls: some with child, some with sickness. Which would my sister come with? As they were able, some moved to a better place. My parents stayed another week in case Fatmata appeared, but still no sister. So we moved to a village close to this camp, where we found a small, abandoned hut with the roof burned off. Dad found a piece of metal, which he secured to the top to keep the rain out. I loved this place. Dad and I walked around and saw plenty of fruit trees—mostly mango. A great coffee tree grew in the middle of the yard, but its smell gave me a headache.

Dad knew the previous owners, as he worked for them before the war. They had told him he was always welcome, so it was okay to eat from whichever trees we liked.

They'd left some pigs in the back of the house, so Dad took care of them so we didn't eat their fruit without helping. He kept the place clean by feeding the pigs and making sure they stayed well.

He also guarded the larger, fancier house they'd left to prevent people from breaking in. I wished I knew what it looked like inside, but they hadn't given Dad permission to enter it, so he wouldn't allow it.

Some days, my dad, mom, and brother would cut down wood in the forest to sell at the market. With the money they made, we bought fish and seasoning to make fruit stew. I never knew you could make so many stews from fruit.

At the market one day, a priest spoke to us and asked if we would like to visit his church. I said, yes. On Sunday, a car picked up my two sisters and me. I was glad he did, because it was a long drive and walking would have taken too long.

The church took place in a beautiful tent. Displayed inside was a picture of a lovely lady holding her baby. She was called Mary, the mother of Jesus. I fell in love with it.

Another picture was of a man, his arms open wide and one of his feet lay on top of the other. Nails held his feet and hands and he looked sad. Because my attention was on this image, I had heard nothing the Father said. All I remembered was the hail Mary prayer. Why was the man pictured like that? What did he do? I didn't like how hurt he looked, but there was something about him I liked.

After church, the priest talked with me. He asked for me and my parents to come see him on Tuesday. He sent a car to pick us up and when we arrived, many people walked about. The priest welcomed us, along with a nurse, who took my weight and height. She also brought me some food to take home and an envelope with money.

The priest told us to come every Tuesday and every time I came; they gave something different, plus money. I was grateful for his great compassion. It helped my family eat well. Mom bought me some new clothes and shoes, and we even bought a gas lamp to help us see at night. I didn't know how he helped all those people, but I hoped to do the same someday for someone in need.

Weeks went by and still my sister hadn't appeared. My parents lost hope and assumed she was dead. They said we needed to move on with our lives. Everyone cried as if we had had a funeral for her. I cried for my mom's loss of a child. Memories of Fatmata, my loving sister, filled my head—all the fun times we had in Moyamba. I didn't even have the chance to say goodbye. We would move on, but it would be one of the hardest journeys for us.

My sisters, brothers, and I still attended church, but our parents never came with us. I never understood why and I never asked them. I assumed it was because it was too far for them to walk.

I loved walking to church with my siblings—the long, dusty road, the summer heat on my skin. Delicious. Some days we took another path where we went through a cornfield and peanut field. I didn't care for this way because I didn't want bugs or snakes jumping at me. We had to run, so the owner didn't catch us. We took other ways, sometimes getting lost, but eventually we found our way back to the main road.

During these long walks, we made up for lost time. We laughed and played games. My brothers and sisters didn't see me any differently. All they saw was their sister, whom they loved very much. I also saw myself that way and played and laughed as if I had lost nothing. Some days I forgot I didn't have hands until I had to be fed and bathed. But it felt different. This was my family, and I was free to be me. I wasn't shy or afraid at all. I felt love all around me.

For a month, all was well. One day, we went to the river to wash our clothes. How I missed those days back in Moyamba! That day felt the same. I laid in the river and let memories flood my mind. I smelled the fragrant rice field and felt the sun's heat, just like I used to. If we returned, I would still remember everything about it. When would I see my sweet home again?

Back in Moyamba, the rebels had burnt everything. Would my parents rebuild? I hoped they would, because this busy village was for those with businesses and a proper education, not farmers. Moyamba was less complicated for those like my parents, who couldn't spell or write their names. We didn't even know our birthdays. We just picked a day that sounded good to us. I didn't love them any less for that. They brought me into this world and they were my parents. I didn't care about what they had or didn't have. To me, my parents were superheroes.

I learned Moyamba was an hour away by car. We were closer than I thought! I asked, "Can we go?"

Dad said, "Not yet. It's not safe. But we can visit family members who live nearby: my mom, my brother, and his wife."

One day, we left for this visit. I loved the walk. With every step, I felt closer to Moyamba. Many fruit trees grew along the way and Dad stopped to pick some for us to eat. These trees are for anyone, so we didn't have to worry. We weren't stealing.

We were happy until we came upon a wide river where we had to cross over on two skinny logs. Who came up with this idea? Two logs? Did they have fantastic balance, unlike me, who needed about a hundred logs? This river flowed straight to the ocean, so if you slipped and fell and couldn't swim, it would be over for you and me.

I lined my feet up at the edge and just ran for it. Somehow, we all made it. We enjoyed visiting the family we hadn't seen for such a long time. They gave us some oil and rice when we left. We needed to stop for breaks because of the extra weight, which made our trip back slower.

Another week later, as our family sat around the fire, we saw someone walking down the road. At first, Mom thought it might be my missing sister, Fatmata. But she returned to cooking, sure it couldn't be. But she stopped again and shaded her eyes with her hand. Mom ran down the road and cried, "It's her, it's her! My baby is here. She's not dead!"

My older sister looked different, not because I hadn't seen her in five years, but because her hands and ankles were swollen. My happiness at seeing her with us overshadowed the sadness I felt about the pain she was in. I wanted to ask about her capture, but was afraid of what she might say. Every time she looked at me, she cried because of my wounds. I said, "Stop crying. I don't like that. It may be hard for you to understand, but just move on from the idea of me not having hands."

Fatmata was sick for a week after she joined us. Mom worried she might be pregnant by the rebels. But after a second week, she felt better. She woke up from nightmares, sometimes screaming with sweat dripping down her body, as if someone was beating her. She was different. The rebels had messed with her head, so all she saw now was them.

They took her purity from her, too. She had tried to fight back, but all she received was a black eye, broken ribs, and a wounded hand. She wished to die, so she didn't have to relive all these bad memories.

I completely understood how helpless she must have felt. People took advantage of her body and she had no power to stop it. She took long showers to wash off their handprints, but it was no use. The trauma left her scarred from within: a scar only she saw and felt.

Some nights, Fatmata and I stayed up and talked about our old lives back in Moyamba, so we didn't fall asleep—and dream. We both had healing to do. I had to learn how to use what I had left while she tried to live one day at a time and understand that what happened to her wasn't her fault.

It was difficult for her. She didn't want to go anywhere, especially if there were guys around. So, she ended up staying in the hut with our mom. I understood, but hoped she eventually would trust again.

Murray Town

One day, I went with my mom and dad to catch a fish. Of course I could do nothing without hands. Discouraged, all I could do was sit and watch them fight with a catfish together. How hard do you have to fight a fish? For it to take two people, it must have been a big one.

Afterward, we visited a garden with vegetables and bought only what we needed: eggplant, onions, and tomatoes. That night, Mom made pepper soup and rice. This was called the poor man's meal, and it was good during cold weather. Lots of spicy peppers helped to fight a cold. It made your nose run like crazy—if it was stuffed up. But none of us was sick. If we were, we'd have been lucky to have the right meal that night.

The following day, a guy came and told my parents they needed to take me to an amputee camp where people like me lived so I could be helped. Help sounded okay, but I liked where I was for now. We stayed.

The next day, I decided to throw myself a birthday party.

Since I didn't know when my birthday was, and my parents didn't remember, I chose that day. Don't ask me what month it was, but I knew it was Saturday.

Mom went to the market and used some of the money the priest had given me. She bought rice, oil, some big fish, Kool-Aid, and fancy spices to make me Jollof. She even made sweet cakes. Not a poor man's meal, this was a wedding kind of food. I dressed up in a fine dress Mom got me. Everything looked and smelled great.

This was the first party for me since I was born. So that day, I told everyone I was eleven. We ate, danced, and played games. It was a terrific day. I'm glad I did it, because it could have been the last time we got together like that.

One sunny afternoon, I played outside with some kids when we saw a white man walking toward us. Where in the world or bush did he come from? We looked around him, but there was no car or anyone else with him.

I remembered seeing some white UN soldiers when they took me to the hospital, and some in the surgery room, but why did this one come and how did he find his way to our remote village, hidden from the outside world?

He walked toward me and spoke, but I couldn't understand his language, except when he said, "Picture," and smiled.

I nodded my head and said, "Yes." He took lots of pictures and went back to wherever he came from.

Another week later, two men came and asked about the amputee camp again. Was I in trouble for not wanting to go?

Mom said, "We can go and if we don't like it, we can come back."

The man said, "I have a booth waiting and the hospital already has it registered to you."

How did that happen? I'm glad my family came with me. It was a light trip: two bags of clothes and a few pots and pans. They drove us for about an hour to Murray Town Camp, in the middle of Freetown. It was close to one of our famous beaches: Lumley Beach.

I remembered coming all the way here to sell for my aunt. Back then, it was beautiful. Now, it stood empty. They transformed one of the larger marketplaces into a camp for the war-wounded. This camp was better than the first camp we lived in, because they built the tiny houses with heavier materials to protect people from the rain and sun.

However, the room was too small for a family of ten. That didn't bother us. Our love for each other was bigger. My family was all I wanted. It didn't matter where we lived, as long as we were together. I was fine with that.

With so many wounded, the place was like the hospital, but without doctors. Some were wounded on the outside while others on the inside. Most didn't want to talk about what the rebels did to them, but some did. One of them told me they were forced to eat someone else's poo and drink their pee. How disgusting! I made friends quickly. Some I remembered from the hospital, like Sia, the girl that got her hand beaten with a hammer. She became one of my best friends. Other girls, I had met at the homeless camp.

We did many things together, including forming a dance group led by one of the camp's leaders. We had four boy drummers. Each weekend, we would compete with other dancers from different camps—we usually won.

They gave us money, but some took offense at that, because the people without hands usually got more than others, especially young kids like me. Sometimes they spoke hatefully about me. They wished I wasn't there. They said I was new, and that many came to see me instead of them, which made them unhappy. Because they had lived there longer, they thought they deserved more.

Their speech and the way they looked at me made me feel bad. I agreed with them. I wish I didn't have my hands severed or the war to have happened. But I didn't understand the hate. I never ran toward the visitors. They always found me and for that, some of the wounded disliked me. Now I hid from visitors. Nightmares kicked in. I dreamed of angry people yelling. In the dream, the entire camp turned against me, threw things at me, and forced us to leave.

One morning, I told my family I wanted to move back to the hut. They spoke with the camp leader, but he told them I needed to stay because it was better for me. I disagreed.

The first few weeks were fine, but now I felt threatened. My nightmares worsened. One night I dreamt someone put snakes in our room to kill us. I woke up sweating and my heart raced and beat faster than a drum. I climbed into my mom's arms and cried. I told her about my dreams, but I never told her what people said. She told me some people didn't want me in the camp. Maybe she saw them, too. Maybe she understood my dreams.

My dad wanted me to stay to see what kind of help I'd receive. So, in the meantime, I tried to stay out of the way. If we had visitors, I stayed in my booth all day. Sometimes the camp leader got angry and sent someone to fetch me. He told me to stop hiding, but I didn't listen. I hid behind someone else's booth and watched everyone being called up to collect their supplies. My name was called, too, but I didn't come out.

Hiding became easy. Sometimes, I asked my sister to take me to the beach. Other days, I hid around the camp. By the end of each day, I'd get my supplies. I only met with those who asked for me. When I walked around the camp, I clearly saw who had problems with me and I avoided getting on their bad side. But I knew not everyone disliked me.

As I sat with my family one day, a group of wounded asked me to go with them to protest to the rebel leader and show him the mess he had made. That made no sense. Why would we want to go there? But my parents thought it might be a good idea.

I wanted to stay, but the protesters insisted I go along. The crazy part was that all the ones without hands got in the front. Were we mad or crazy? I saw the look in some of their eyes: They were angry at the rebels and the war they created.

I hoped we didn't start another war. Some meant well:

They had heard the rebel leader would speak to the people to make peace with them and the president. That's why most were going.

As we walked, our group got bigger and bigger. Thirsty and tired, I wanted to turn back, but slowed down instead, until I was at the back of the line. I didn't care.

Halfway, some people ran back. Some cried and blood flowed from their heads or other places. I wasn't sure, but I guessed the rebel leader didn't want to see or speak to them, after all. Immediately, I turned around and headed back to the camp. Gunshots fired and people ran for their lives and cried. A lady passed me and asked if I had been close enough to see any people killed. I said, "No."

I wished I'd never come on this trip. My parents were probably worried that I was dead. If anyone ever asked me to do something like this again, I would just say no, thank you.

Back at the camp, my sister ran, crying, toward me. The protesters returned and now realized they needed to let things be. I didn't want to fight or look for those that hurt me or my sister. I wanted to play kid games with my friends and keep moving forward.

Many times, people have asked if I knew the people that cut off my hands. I always answer, no, because I don't want to talk about it.

While walking around the camp one day, I regarded the wounded people. A mother with both of her legs cut off had four children to take care of. A dad without both of his hands and his wife with one hand, who needed to take care of their children, but now their children took care of them. How could these kids have time to be kids if they were taking care of their parents?

My sister did the same for me. I can't have her do that forever. She had been helpful and patient with me. She woke up with me and took me to the washroom and helped me dress. So, one day I fed myself. It wasn't easy, but I did it. And I showered myself. I did well with the front, but needed help with the back. I would try every day until I got it right.

New Hands?

Months later, I got news from my aunt that she wanted to see me. My parents were firmly against it, but I wanted to tell her I had no hate for her in my heart. By the look on my parent's faces, they never wanted me to see her again. Instead of asking one of them to come with me, I ended up asking Jama, my younger sister, to join me. My parents insisted that I not stay with her. I told them I knew better. I just wanted to know why she sent for me.

To be honest, I wasn't looking forward to it. On our way, I showed my sister where I used to sell things and where I fetched water. I loved the memories of walking along this road to church with my cousin Beria.

I thought back to when she and I had attended church and met my uncle. The entire church had felt sorry for what the war did to me; they had even raised money for me. That was very generous. I had felt rich that day: all that money was for me, so my cousin and I stopped and bought lots of snacks. After that, we still had money left. Carrying that much money made me afraid.

I remembered that we gave some away to others that looked like they needed it so Aunt Dankey didn't think I had stolen it. But, we still had some money left. We tried to eat all the snacks before we reached the house, which was funny because then we hid the leftovers. Some snacks were in my drawers and some in hers. We had laughed so hard that day, people looked at us like we were crazy. If only they had known.

But now, Jama and I went the back way so I could show her where they cut off my hands. The stone was still there. I felt the pain all over again, so we left. When we got to the house, Aunt Dankey smiled. She had made dinner for us, too. My ability to feed myself surprised everyone. My cousin Beria and I were happy to meet again. I missed her very much. Beria said she was going to stay with her mom. That was good, because she didn't look well—like she'd lost a lot of weight.

Dankey talked about life before the war. "I've missed having you around. Have you missed it, too?"

"Yes," I said.

"Would you like to come back and live here?" she asked.

I looked at my sister and my cousin and said, "I can't because I must live in the camp with others like me." My aunt's and cousin's faces fell. "I don't want to hurt anyone, but I don't think there is anything more for me here. I'm not sure if there's much at the camp either, but I need to stay with my family."

Dankey said, "You look different."

She acted like she wanted to say something, but couldn't. Her eyes said she was sorry, which made me feel sorry, too, but I didn't know for what. When our time was up, we said our goodbyes and she asked me to come see her again.

On the way home, we stopped by the house where I used to live with my aunt, uncle, and cousin. The place looked fine, but the rebels took most of the pigs that used to live there.

I learned the rebels had shot and killed the owner of the place. Tears ran down my face. He was such a kind man. My heart went out to his family. I wanted to walk around the place, but it was all too sad.

So, we stopped by the church, but it wasn't open. I would have loved to go in and sit for a while. Maybe I'd find Jesus, or he'd find me. After all, this was the place where I first heard about him. Something about today drove me toward him. But where could you look for someone so powerful? Why was he hiding from us?

I had so many questions. The sun was setting, so we pressed on to meet the bus, which took us back to the camp. We made it and it was good to be back. It wasn't a homey type of place, but better than nothing.

They placed a church in the center of the camp. Every morning around 4:00, very catchy music came from there. I was curious, but didn't want to visit uninvited, so I sat on the veranda and listened to the beautiful sounds. Their voices were so pure and sweet. Oh, I wished I could sing like that for Jesus. I would sing until I saw him and touched him.

After the music ended, I went back inside, but couldn't go back to sleep. Jesus was on my mind. If I saw him, would he look like the pictures in the Bible? I didn't know, but the image of him in my heart looked even better than these pictures. Either way, I didn't care. I loved him.

Soon I hung posters of him on my plastic walls, the door, and the window. I loved the look of the room now.

When the sun rose, a boy walked through the camp and knocked on doors to invite people up for church, but he didn't come to my door. Why? I came out to listen to the music. Some words I understood, but some I didn't because they sang them in a different language. Still, they were comforting. Could Jesus understand them?

The next morning, I woke up early to sit outside. Maybe the boy would see me and invite me to church. He passed by and said nothing. Disappointed, I hung my head. Why didn't he ever come to my booth?

Inside, I lay down by my grandma and she rubbed my back. **Knock, knock.** Someone was at the door! I opened it and it was the boy with his lamp asking if I wanted to come to church. I gave him a broad smile and said, "Yes!".

Grandma went with me. We sang and danced to the songs we knew and listened to the pastor speak. Thank goodness he spoke Krio. I understood, but I had to translate the message to Grandma.

After church, the boy came over to talk to Grandma and me. He asked, "Do you know Jesus?"

I said, "I've heard stories about him, but my grandma hasn't."

He smiled. "Do you want to know about him?"

Grandma grinned and said, "Yes."

"Why?" the boy asked.

"Because he sounds interesting," Grandma said.

The boy talked with her for a long time and she liked everything he said about Jesus. She told me we would go every morning so she could learn more. So every morning, we got ready before he came knocking. The camp started having morning services every day, which I loved.

I realized the boy who knocked was one of the drummers from our dance group. I had paid little attention to the drummers while I danced. He played the drums at church. His dad was the pastor. He must have had a busy life. He was one of the few kids in the camp that had nothing wrong with them, but I learned his mom was wounded in the war.

After the dance one day, he told me he liked me. I didn't know what to think about that. He shocked me. Why would anyone like me, especially without hands? So I didn't respond. Later that day, he came by my booth and talked with Grandma to see how she was doing.

That night, Grandma gave her heart to Jesus and became a Christian. My heart bounced with joy to know someone else in my family was in love with Jesus.

The next day, some specialists came into the camp to take measurements of the amputees. Could they make us hands and legs? They gave me a velcro wrap to hook a spoon on, which made feeding myself easier.

Next, I would receive hook hands. I hoped they would be easy for me to use. I had seen some using them already. They made it look effortless. They called me for another measurement somewhere else. Finally, they gave me a hook hand, which I loved. It wasn't easy to use, but if I practiced enough, I would get the hang of it.

While I was at the prosthetics place, I made a new friend, Hawa. Her hands were both cut off, and she was also from the same tribe as me. I invited her to come to the camp where she could be helped. She was friendly, and I liked her. The other girls at the camp would, too.

We had another dance competition; it was a long one, and we didn't return to camp until 10:00 at night. I loved dancing. It made me feel normal. Sometimes I forgot about the war or living in a camp.

While I sat with Grandma, the same man who took pictures of me when I was ten came to our booth. This time, he introduced himself and I wasn't afraid. By now, I was used to people coming and going from the camp. He asked to take more pictures of me as I fed myself and played with friends. I was comfortable with him. He liked my family and enjoyed playing soccer with the boys. He even took pictures of people braiding hair. The kids loved him because he was fun to be around.

Forgiveness

One day, they told us the president would come to visit the camp, and we would perform for him. We practiced our dance over and again, so we got it just right. Everyone loved having him, and he enjoyed his visit. We put on quite a show and our guests threw money on the floor as we danced. It was the most excitement we'd ever had in our camp.

Just when things couldn't get any better, we were told we'd have more people coming to show us a movie. Not just any movie, but a Jesus movie. Were they joking? I could bust from excitement! Over the years, I'd heard about the Jesus movie, and finally I would have the chance to see it.

I got ready for the movie like I would meet Jesus in person. I ate, took a shower, and even put on my finest dress. Then I waited. I wanted it to grow dark already, so the movie would start.

Workers lined up rows of chairs for us in the theatre area, and soon the people with the movie came. I brought my family and a blanket with me. At last it started. Jesus spoke in Krio! I had been afraid he wouldn't know how to speak my language, so I was glad.

I enjoyed every part of the movie except when some people started not liking him. Why were they trying to kill him, no matter what he did? I got furious. I didn't like these people. They acted like the rebels that killed and maimed people for no good reason. Jesus did nothing wrong, but they wanted him dead. They beat him, spat on him, and dragged him across the floor. With every lash of the whip, his skin tore open. His eyes were sorrowful.

I couldn't watch any more. I was so mad I cried and screamed for them to stop. Just when I thought they had finished whipping him, they took Jesus, laid him on a cross, and began nailing his hands. Inside, I hurt so much I cried. Almost the entire audience turned around to look at me. One lady who brought the movie came and pulled me onto her lap to explain things. "Jesus is fine. You need to keep watching because something good is about to happen."

"Why did they beat him like that?" I asked.

She said, "Because he loves you. He came to die for you and everyone so that we may know how much he loves us. And he wants us to love each other just like he loves you, and to be good—even to the people who are not good to us."

I watched as they lifted the cross. Tears ran down my face. That much love surprised me. He went through all that just to show his love. How could I not love him back? As he hung on the cross, he prayed for the people that put him there. While he hung, they made fun of him. Moreover, they put a crown of thorns on his head and gambled for his robe. Yet, he still loved us.

He prayed a forgiveness prayer for them, so I wanted to love and forgive like him. I would start with the rebels, my aunt, and the kids that falsely accused me of stealing. I vowed I would forgive for as long as I live.

The movie showed the sadness of people who loved him. Even the sky! Clouds covered the sky, darkening it. The sound of thunder came, followed by rain. During that time, Jesus died. Then the sky cleared up.

A stillness settled over the camp. People sniffed from crying. The movie continued. They took Jesus' body down and wrapped him in burial clothes. I was numb with sadness and wished he hadn't died.

Those that loved him were depressed and missed him. I missed him too, and I wasn't even there. I stood and picked up my blanket to return to my booth. But why were people still sitting? I heard someone say, "Look, he is gone!"

What? The movie wasn't over? So I sat down again. Where did they move him? No one did. His wrappings were still there, but his body wasn't. Then, there he was, standing in the middle of his friends and disciples. The camp went mad. We screamed, clapped, and cheered. I couldn't believe it: My savior, my redeemer, my maker lives!

I had seen nothing more powerful than this. Jesus is so strong and mighty that even death couldn't hold him down. For the next couple of days, I felt something inside change. No longer was I mad at the rebels—I was sorry for them. I gained a love for my aunt. Not only that, I prayed for everyone who had ever wronged me. Now I felt lighter and free inside—able to smile and feel like a kid again.

I wasn't sure why, but at that time, many asked me, "What do you think of the war and the rebels?"

Well, let me tell you, these were not good questions for me. What did they want me to say? That the rebels did a very good job? Or perhaps, it wasn't that bad? It *WAS* bad! I wished the rebels had known Jesus so they wouldn't have done what they did. But it was over now and I had forgiven them. I was letting God take over. And I hoped they found Jesus, even now.

Life in the camp became stressful. Guests not only took pictures, but some came to take kids overseas to help them, if their family approved. Lucky for me, I was one kid on this list, but I didn't know if I wanted to leave my family again.

Depressed about it, I hid from the camp leader. This time, he scolded my parents for allowing me to hide. Some people wondered if I didn't want help. They made fun of me for not being one of the many kids who were going overseas. Their words hurt, so I told them I would go to America soon, so they would stop teasing me.

One day, I received a huge box stuffed with goodies: pictures of a beautiful family, another picture of them standing outside with trees covered with pretty white stuff, clothes, money, and a letter from Louis Landry in Canada.

I took the letter and pictures to a guy in the camp who could read it to me. Maybe he could tell me what the white stuff was on the trees, too. He said the letter was a message of hope and love. These people who I didn't know said prayers for me and sent me money. The white stuff was called snow.

I loved this family so much; I wanted to meet them. I carried their pictures everywhere I went and hoped someday we would meet. The same guy who read the letter helped me write a thank you note back to them. In it, I gave them my love and expressed my gratefulness for the wonderful stuff.

One gorgeous afternoon, I kicked a soccer ball around with my friends. A group of people at the camp leader's booth talked with a white man. He was looking for someone. I stood far away from everyone else, but I heard him say my name: Mariatu.

I didn't think he was asking for me because there was another Mariatu at the camp and her hands were cut off, too. But it wasn't her he was looking for. He showed a group of people in the camp a picture, and they knew it was me.

They brought me to him. As soon as he saw me, he smiled and spoke, but I couldn't understand his words. Someone else translated them.

I asked, "Where did he get this picture?"

The translator asked the white man and then told me, "He saw it in Time magazine."

He was going to help me in any way possible. My interpretation was that I would go to America. There was something about him I liked. I trusted he wouldn't lie to me, even when he told me he must return to America. He said he would be back and then he would take me with him.

I didn't know why, but I wasn't afraid to move to another country without my family anymore. Maybe it was because my family trusted him, too. All I cared to do now was wait for his return.

More kids moved overseas, but I still waited. Some told me to go on with other kids, but I didn't want to. Even my parents had doubts because it had been a few months. I held onto my faith.

He finally came back with a pastor in late October, 1999. I was ecstatic to see him and told him so in my language. He asked, "What is she saying?"

The pastor translated for him. "She said she knew you would come back."

The man said, "God told me to come back. Lots of people from our church are praying for you."

I felt so lucky to have people I didn't know praying for me in another country. And I was thrilled that God told him to return.

The next day I was with a friend when the white man and pastor came. They said, "I can take you and your friend, Sia, with me to America and help you both, if you and your parents allow it." I nodded. Then he spoke through the pastor to my parents. "She can talk to you when she's in America, and she can come back to visit. Are you okay with that?" They were. I had mixed emotions. I was happy, but part of me was sad about leaving my family again. The pain I was feeling from leaving this time differed from the first time in Moyamba because I wasn't being forced into it.

I saw I needed some help and agreed to receive this gift—one everyone hoped for in this camp. Sia, coming with me, helped a little. The next day, everything moved quickly. There were legalities to take care of. At the Embassy, we had passport pictures taken. A sweet lady who was a social worker filled out paperwork for us and made sure we would go to the United States. That took time, as there were a lot of papers to go through.

It was nearly dinnertime when we got back to the camp, and we were running out of time. I had to find someone to do my hair. I wished there was more time. The hairstyle I wanted would take three hours to do and I wouldn't have enough time to spend with my family. So I chose the wash and jell style. Usually, this turned out fine, but that day my hair looked like a big blob on my head.

I had no time to complain, as we had to leave first thing in the morning. For dinner, Mom made my favorite dish: bean stew and rice. Before bedtime, I said goodbye to my friends. When I returned home, I curled up in Mom's arms like I was a baby again and took in all the love I could.

I slept some but got up very early. I sat and watched my family bunched up together, sleeping on the floor. They were a little closer now, because Mom had another baby. Though she took up little space, everyone was careful not to roll on my new sister.

I tried to go back to sleep but couldn't. I lay my head on my mom's chest and listened to her heartbeat: regular and peaceful. Mine beat faster. Maybe I was nervous. I sat outside for a while and studied the stars. Would the same stars shine in America, too? If so, I would see the same stars as my family.

I walked back inside and slept some more. Mom woke me up so I could shower, get ready, and eat. I packed nothing because they told me someone already had things for me and Sia. My family and I hugged and said prayers before the pastor and the white man came to pick us up.

It was time. The pastor and white man took us and my dad to a taxi, which waited at the end of the camp. Dad rode with us to the boat and ferry station, where we took pictures for my family to keep, plus some for us taken with another camera. The goodbye was painful, but they wanted me to go. So did I. It was good to hear my dad say he was not sad, but happy I was getting help. The great thing is that the pastors would help us communicate with our parents.

Coming to America

Watching the ferry move from side to side made me sick. I had been told stories that a creature in the sea would rise to tip over boats and ships—what about a ferry? Was it bigger or safer?

While I stood and worried, cars lined up to drive onto the ferry. We did that too. Would we sink because of the weight of the cars? Could we swim back if we were trapped in the car? Remember, I couldn't swim and I was already seasick from the ferry's movements.

I closed my eyes and sang songs from Sunday School to calm me, which helped.

On the ferry, we stepped out of the car, and the pastor handed us some food he had brought along. "Here's your first American meal. A cheeseburger."

It smelled good. I took off the top of the bun, removed the lettuce, tomatoes, and pickles, and ate just the meat and bread. They laughed, but I hoped all the food wasn't like this. I prayed America would have rice.

I asked Sia, "Are you worried about moving to America?"
She smiled. "Not as much as you, I think."

It's terrible that she saw this on my face.

She continued. "You must stop worrying and be more grateful."

"But I am," I said. "Just homesick." Why didn't she feel homesick like I did? Oh, well. Now I needed to remember what the pastor told us about the white man's family in America. He had two kids: a boy and a girl. We would call his wife, Mom, and him we would call Dad. The pastor had said we must get used to calling him Dad because we would live with them. Because of language differences, it was easy to call them this. In my native tongue, Temne, we had nicknames for our parents.

The ferry finally stopped. I would never ride on that again. Oh, but I would if I ever wanted to visit my family again. Thinking about it made me queasy. The pastor walked us to a building with airplanes around it.

"This is as far as I can go," he said.

Was he joking? No. How were we going to communicate with someone who didn't speak our language?

"Don't worry. I've taught him a few basic words in Krio. You'll do just fine." We learned a few important words in English, too: food, bathroom, please, and thank you. That was all we needed to know for now.

Traveling to America was proving dangerous. First a ferry and now an airplane. I didn't know I was afraid of heights until I got on the plane. My heart beat faster and I felt there wasn't enough air on the plane for me to breathe. As the plane took flight, my stomach dropped. I guessed it was too late to ask to get off. Besides, the white man wouldn't understand me.

I had a window seat, so I watched the size of everything on the ground shrink, including the people. The higher we were, the smaller it all got. I was sorry I sat by the window. Later, all I saw was clouds, and I didn't feel safe. I changed seats with Sia, closed my eyes, and sang. I let the song take me back to when Jesus was in the boat with his disciples. I knew if anything went wrong, he would be here with us.

The plane landed in Lagos, Nigeria, and I was thankful we were on the ground again. In the airport, the white man ordered a meal of eggs and ham with a side of buttered toast. This was the best tasting food I'd had since we left Sierra Leone—until the waiter brought a bowl full of a cold and tasty orange-flavored treat. I later learned this was a frozen sherbet. I might survive after all.

Now we boarded another plane. This one is larger than the first, with more passengers and a longer ride. We landed in the Ivory Coast and stayed a few days with a family. The lady of the house was friendly and hospitable. She welcomed us with open arms, as if she expected us. I loved the fact that she spoke Krio. She asked, "Who did your hair like this?"

We laughed because we knew it was crazy.

"You can take a shower and wash it, if you like. I'll braid your hair."

She walked us to the washroom. I had never seen anything this beautiful in my life. They had a big tub you sat in to wash and a shower big enough for three people. They never had to worry about fetching water, for it was already in the house.

"Which would you like to use: the bathtub or the shower?" she asked.

We picked the shower because we had never sat in a tub before to wash. She showed us how to use the handles and we showered. The water was already warm, so we didn't have to wait for a fire to warm it. I enjoyed every drop of water on my head. It was like washing under the rain, but warm. I ended the shower because I didn't want to waste water.

Afterward, she brushed and braided our hair nicely and added beads at the ends. The next day, we shopped and bought some beautiful dresses and shoes. On our way back to the house, many people greeted us in French. That was fun, so we practiced a few words our host taught us. She was pleasant to be around.

She surprised us by making cassava leaf stew and rice for dinner. It tasted just like home and the smell of it made me miss it and my family.

Depressed and homesick inside, these feelings made me embarrassed. They never forced me to go to America. This was a chance everyone wanted back in the camp. *Lord, please don't let me be ungrateful,* I prayed.

I loved the kindness offered since we arrived, but I worried we might not make it to America. Every time the white man left us for a moment, fear grew inside me. I was so afraid, I asked the lady, "Will the white man leave us here?" She saw how worried I was and spoke of it to the white man.

He got on his knees and said, "I will never leave you. We are leaving for America tomorrow."

What a relief! He still wanted us and no matter what, he would make sure we got to America, with God's help. That night I slept well, knowing this was our last stop before we would be on American soil.

The big day came. We wore our beautiful dresses and our pretty hairstyles. I had to say; we looked and felt attractive.

We said our goodbyes with thankful hearts. We took pictures, hopped into the car, and drove away. At the airport, the planes were even larger than either of the first two. You might think I would be used to flying by now, but that wasn't true. I was still afraid of heights. The only thing that kept me sane was my faith. I knew God wouldn't allow anything bad to happen on this plane.

This plane flew higher than the last one. My ears played hide and seek with me: one would pop and the other would close. The more anxious I became about getting to America, the longer the trip got.

Maybe if I fell asleep, time would pass quickly. But how could you sleep sitting up straight? That was impossible for me, but not for some. Many other passengers were already fast asleep.

How did they do it? They made it look easy, although some looked like their necks might break. Others looked like they were laying in beds or a comfy chair. I guessed they must travel a lot, so they were used to it.

It had been more than an hour of sitting on my butt. I couldn't feel it much anymore, nor my feet. If I had my hands, would they be numb, too? I tried leaning from one side to the other, which was difficult buckled in a seatbelt. Sitting sloppy like a fish didn't help either. I think the seats made you learn to sit properly, like a lady. I remembered all the times my grandma tried to fix my posture. She would've gotten a kick at seeing me like this. She might say, "Now you have no choice but to sit like a lady."

Using the bathroom on the plane was something I didn't want to do often. I had to unfasten my belt, walk between people, and the flushing of the toilet was strong enough to suck you right out of the plane.

The flight was long, and I grew too tired to fight it anymore. Somehow I slept for about twenty minutes. I was proud of that.

Some passengers watched a funny movie. The white man put the same movie on for us. I couldn't believe how many gadgets this plane had. First, a mini-table folded down from the back of the seat in front of us. A lady served food and drinks, and now we watched a TV of our own. The movie was called *Big Mama's House*. We had no idea what they said, but we laughed at their movements and action. I even forgot I was on a plane!

I wasn't sure how long our flight was, but I enjoyed the last hour of it because of the snacks and the movie. I'm happy we landed on the ground and hoped I knew how to use my legs again, since they were numb. We landed in another country this time: Belgium. To stretch our legs, we walked and visited some shops. We bought some snacks and ate. People were everywhere: some hurried and pulled suitcases behind them, while others took their time.

Our wait was over and we stood in line to go through security for another plane ride. I got used to the idea of boarding, but that didn't mean I liked it. Every time the plane took off, my stomach dropped. This ride was just as long as the last, and I was thankful for it. Later in the flight, I told Sia, "I think we are in America. I can't wait to get to the house so I can lie on my belly and the other parts of my body can rest."

She laughed. "You're acting like you're broken."

I said, "You're lucky I don't have hands. I'd pinch you just to make sure you have feelings."

We headed back to another waiting station. Just when I thought the ride was over, we headed for *another* plane. To be honest, my body was so tired, I wanted to cry. It was dark outside now. All you saw were lights outside the window, but they were lovely. The sparkling lights overwhelmed me. Instead of watching movies to waste time, I kept myself busy with looking out of the window. What was better than that was that this ride was shorter than the last two. We were here. We were finally here!

I didn't know we were a big deal until we left the plane. A crowd of people clapped, cheered, and said, "Welcome to America!" Our American family and friends held up signs, balloons, and teddy bears. People I've never met welcomed us with such excitement and warmth. From that moment, I felt loved and taken care of. I was thrilled, but even more so when I saw some Sierra Leonians in the welcome group.

We left the airport and went out to eat. I cried for my family back home when I saw how much food was on the table. They never had this much food. I was more exhausted than hungry because of the long trip. I ate bits and pieces, but I wasn't fully aware of my surroundings; like being half awake and half asleep. Someone picked me up and carried me, I remember.

The next morning dawned. When I woke, I was amazed to find everything was in the house: the bathroom, shower, and even the kitchen. Mom helped me start the bath, and I climbed into the warm water with thick bubbles. I almost fell asleep in my first bath. Mom made us a breakfast of eggs and ham just like we'd had in Belgium, but much better. Sia and I loved her cooking, but that wasn't all. She was sweet, kind, and beautiful with her long silky hair. She was always there, ready to help us whenever we needed her.

Communication was difficult with our new parents. We had lots to say, but didn't have the language to say it. But they knew some families from Sierra Leone that lived in the United States, which was of enormous benefit. They visited and brought some African food for us and helped us learn basic English words. Often, the Sierra Leonians came by to see how we progressed. I felt lucky to have a family that wanted to help us. My prayer and hope was that God would bless them more than they had blessed us.

Life in America

There was much to learn about America. First, the weather was different. Here, there are four seasons: winter, spring, summer, and fall. In Sierra Leone, there are only two: rainy and dry. I believed Sierra Leonians might die if they had seasons like this, considering how many caught minor colds in the subtropics. That showed me how great God is: he placed different seasons in various places in the world for people to adapt to. My hope is not to learn to love this weather, but to survive it.

As I walked around my American parents' large property, I saw some beautiful horses running freely. Did they feel the cold? I'd never been close to a horse before. They were even better close up. I got to feed them and feel the soft hair on their skin. Apparently, they could be ridden, too, but I preferred to stay low to the ground. Someday, I might have the courage to ride one.

Inside, I sat by the warm fire. I was amazed by the fire being in the house without burning it down! Dad gave us a tasty, cold treat in a bowl. I loved it. It was like what we had after the first plane trip: sherbet. But this was milky and called ice cream.

Just when I didn't think things could get any more mysterious, they did. Outside the window, I watched white stuff coming down from the sky. I showed Sia, and we wondered what it was: sugar or salt? But the way it looked against the window, we decided it must be coconut flakes.

We went outside and were colder than before. Okay, now neither of us knew what it was. We put some in our mouth. It was cold and melted quickly. I loved the way it fell peacefully on the ground and how it covered up the trees. Then I remembered the pictures with the white stuff on the trees I received back home.

Mom brought a bowl out and scooped some into it. She said it was ice. We brought it in and made ice cream from it. It wasn't bad at all. It tasted something like the ice cream we'd had earlier. Not only could you eat it, but you could slide on it, too. You could slip and fall hard, as well.

I was thankful for the double layer of clothes Mom put on us to cover up my skinny bones and keep me warm. I didn't think I had enough meat to face this cold. When we arrived, I weighed only eighty pounds. At my age, thirteen or fourteen, that wasn't enough. But after a few months, I felt bump, which means fat in Krio. And being fat is good.

I enjoyed learning more basic words and some harder ones in English, thanks to Mom's friend. She took time each day to come by and teach us. Honestly, the English language is very confusing and complicated. There are so many phrases for just one word. The other thing is, they put extra letters in them they don't even use. When I learned to read, I said the words the way I saw them spelled. For example, knee (kuh-nee) and knife (kuh-nife). I knew it wouldn't be easy to learn the English language when I looked at words like this and listened to how fast people spoke. Thank goodness I had nothing else to do but learn.

One day, we visited the doctor. Let me just say that didn't go well. My sister got a needle put in her arm. I leaped for the door and screamed. How many people did the doctors and nurses have to chase down, just so they could give them a shot? Probably not that many. There was just something about being in a hospital building that made me sick every time. My fear had me so worked up, I made myself sick.

Bad news. The bones had grown again on both of my arms and Sia's arm needed an operation. The good news was that Dad had a friend who was very good at this kind of work. People trusted and respected him for his talents.

We had met the surgeon's family before and they opened their home to us, making us feel welcome right away. Their love was contagious, and we always had so much fun with their kids. Their house became our second home.

We even attended church together. This was the same church where a group of Sunday School people met and prayed for people like Sia and me. I was thankful for this family, the church, and the small room where all the prayers came from. This church had some of the world's kindest people. Knowing that, I was sure that this doctor would be the best one to do our surgeries.

All went well with my surgery. The next fun part would be taking out the stitches. How many people would I take down with me? Man, I was such a chicken when it came down to pain. I doubted I would ever get used to it.

Speaking of chicken, one day we went to the supermarket to buy groceries for dinner. I'd never seen such a large place! I tried to wrap my head around all of it. Every part of the store had something different and exciting to see. I had so much fun just walking around; I forgot why we were there. My favorite section was the food side. I saw all the fruits and vegetables we don't have back home, and I was happy to see the ones I was familiar with, too.

Back at the house, Mom got a box of rice out. It was already half-cooked, so it was done in no time. It seemed unnatural for rice to cook that fast. I was used to waiting thirty minutes for rice to fully cook. Was this rice real? It wasn't bad, but it wasn't the best either.

It was time Sia and I tried other foods, so we did. Some things I liked and some I wasn't decided about. Pizza was one food everyone in America loved. I didn't understand why. I tried to like it but couldn't appreciate it. Maybe it's the type I had or the place I had it, but it was covered with too much sauce and cheese: two things my body wasn't familar with. If you asked me, I think they went a little crazy with the sauce and cheese.

Maybe that's how the American people liked it, but I preferred rice. I was sure my mouth would come to love new things as I explored American food.

Our sister, Lacy, came home from college, which was always fun. She had new things to show and teach us. I wished she and our brother, Lucas, lived closer so we could see them every day. Lucas and his wife lived six to eight hours away, so that couldn't be helped. But when we visited them, there were always many fun things to do.

The first holiday we celebrated at Lucas's was Thanksgiving. It made no sense to me. You cooked many foods all day and everyone ate until no one could eat anymore. After that, you played games and ate some more. Why? I didn't remember having this holiday back home in Africa. But I liked it a lot. I especially enjoyed the game we played called Mafia. It was intense! I looked forward to it whenever we visited. Never a dull moment with them.

Next, we enrolled in school. My stomach dropped, and my head spun, and I wasn't even a moving object. Happiness and fear caused my head and stomach to panic. Our first day went well, but the class was too advanced for us. Because of our lack of schooling, they placed us into smaller classes so we could catch up. Our teachers were patient and understanding, which I loved.

The only thing I wasn't crazy about was waking up early to catch the bus to school. At least I dozed off with half of the other kids on the bus before we reached the school.

Riding home on the bus was crazy. You'd think the kids would be tired from all their hard work, but no. They acted like they had drunk two cups of sugar water.

I felt sorry for our bus driver for having to listen to all that. I tried to catch a nap, but couldn't close my eyes. Oh well, at least I didn't have to go to the market to sell things or fetch water for the house when I got home.

As much as I loved school, I also loved getting home to spend time with Mom and Dad and help them pack boxes to send to countries that needed help. They sent some boxes to Sierra Leone as well. It was a lot of work and many volunteered to help. The place was always full of fun and laughter. Helping others was so much fun.

I remembered the last time we helped Dad pack boxes to take to Africa with him. He came back with more kids: two boys and one girl. When I saw the girl, I was thrilled! She was the girl I had run into back home in Africa when I got fitted for my hook hands. Now, I couldn't believe she was here with us. When we three girls got together, we were as crazy as can be. I loved being here with them. Who would Dad bring home next time?

We worked hard, but on the days we didn't, we just ate and watched cars drive by. It was so quiet. Back home in Africa, cars always honked, dogs barked, and kids yelled as they played. Once we called my family and it was so noisy, I spent most of the time saying "Hello, hello. Can you hear me?" Each time, noise overlapped about half of our conversation. I knew it sounded crazy, but sometimes I missed the noise a little.

Finally came the day they would fit my prosthetic hands. It was hard to write at school with the hook hands when the paper kept moving around, even though the teachers tried to help. It would be nice to have something that looked like proper hands.

The process of making them was difficult and would take time, but I couldn't wait. I wanted to feel them, eat with them, to write, and, most importantly, to feel like a normal person. I liked who I was as a person, but I didn't like the way I looked. People stared at me when they walked by. Sometimes, I hid my hands, so they didn't stare. Going out in public was hard for me. I always felt like I was hiding. It wasn't fun for me to be in the open with people I wasn't comfortable with.

When I finally got my prosthetic hands, I was the happiest girl in the world. I loved everything about them. I even bought some rings and bracelets to make them look beautiful. Then, the battery in the left hand broke. Dad took it in to be fixed, which meant I had to go to school with only one of them. I was more embarrassed than anything.

At that moment, I realized I had been hiding behind my hands all this time. With them, I felt good. Without them, I was just the girl with no hands. I made it through the week without the left hand, and I didn't die.

Friends & Family

Just when I thought things couldn't improve, I received a letter:

> Dear Isatu,
>
> I heard you are in the States and you are living with some wonderful family. I'm very happy for you and your friend. I am writing to you because I wanted to see if you and your family would like to come visit me and my family here in Canada. If yes, I will have everything taken care of.
>
> Yours sincerely,
> Louis Landry

When I read this, I couldn't believe it. I jumped for joy! It was all happening so fast. When I lived in Africa, I always dreamed of meeting his family one day. Now that I was in America, I didn't think it would be possible.

But here I stood today, with an invitation to meet them. I had no words to describe the joy I felt right then. Mom and Dad drove the long distance, but it was fun. Many times, we stopped to enjoy the beauty on the way. We even stopped to see Niagara Falls. We saw all kinds of trees: some big, some small. I smelled pine fragrance in the air.

As much as I loved the trip, I longed to reach our destination. Canada is such a beautiful place. I read road signs along the way. One of my favorites was Bienvene. It means welcome. I learned that word from the Ivory Coast.

Finally, we arrived. Everything was just as I had imagined: beautiful and breathtaking. We met the Landry family. They were wonderful, inside and out.

Our time at Louis's was never dull because we did something fun every day. I can't forget the one day we rode in a speedboat. It was scary, but fun at the same time. After the boat ride, we bought some lobster and shrimp to take back to the house. This lobster was enormous!

After dinner, we put on a show for everyone. We sang and showed them some of our African dance moves. Our stay was unbelievable. If it was a dream, I hoped no one would wake me.

Our time in Canada was amazing. We had so many adventures: a visit to the beach, shopped at the mall to buy whatever we wanted, dressed up to go to a ball, and we saw some houses and a chapel building made from different colored wine glasses.

This time was priceless. How could I ever repay their generosity? I didn't think I ever could, but I prayed for God to have a special place in heaven for this family.

Just before we left, we toured Prince Edward Island, where they filmed Anne of Green Gables—my favorite movie, ever. I thought I might burst with excitement. Just like the movie, it was green and gorgeous. We even got to watch a play of Anne.

Sadly, we said goodbye, but I knew we would see the Landry's again. Later, we did return for another visit and I am forever blessed to know this wonderful family.

We had a big weekend back home at church. Some church members came to the office and played some live music. We ate good food and packed more boxes for overseas. And, it was special because we met a wonderful family with two girls. We fell in love with them. Sometimes we stayed overnight on some of our visits to their house. We ate dinner and watched movies. They treated us like family. The girls treated us like sisters.

Later that month, Mom and Dad planned on moving, but Sia and I didn't like that idea. We'd have to switch schools, and we loved the one we attended. We asked if we could stay with this new family with the two girls. so we could at least finish out the school year.

Luckily for us, they said yes. At the end of the school year, we were more in love with them, and their love for us was just as big. Before long, there was talk about adoption. One idea was that one of us stayed with the new family, while the other stayed with our missionary parents.

I didn't want to separate from Sia, and neither family really wanted that scenario either. The next thing I knew, we had two sets of parents who loved us very much. Our home was with the new family, but anytime we wanted, we could visit our missionary parents. Both families loved and spoiled us.

Time marched on and four hormonal girls with attitudes surrounded our newest mom. I didn't know how she coped, but I'm thankful for her and the strength that God gave her. She would be the definition of strength.

One day I stayed after school to try out for track. It went pretty well, but I didn't do much. The next day was great. We worked hard, at least that's what I thought, because the next day I hurt all over—even in places I didn't think could. To help with the soreness, I had to plunge into a tub filled with ice water. Man, I hoped I wouldn't have to do this ever again, but it helped loosen up my muscles. I loved track, but I wasn't interested in the competitive side of it.

After a year of track, I met the boy who would become my husband during practice. I hadn't even seen his face, and I already knew I loved him. His calf muscles attracted me! I said to my friend, "I like him."

She said, "You're crazy. You don't even know what he looks like or anything about him."

"I don't care. After practice, I'm going to talk to him." And I did. Boy, was I glad I liked his calves, because he was very handsome and I loved how nice he was to me and my friend, Debbie.

I asked him, "Would you like to go with me to the play Guys and Dolls at school?"

He agreed and when he picked me up, he was carrying a rose. I was lucky and blessed to meet someone like him—someone who loves me for who I am and not what I look like. Only a true man of God could love someone like me.

Some people ask what makes him love me, which hurts. Did they mean to be rude or something else? Their comments make me feel unworthy of any guy. Their question stings, because I want people to treat me like a normal person. I should be able to fall in love and have kids without feeling shame for the way I look.

The way my husband always answers this horrible question makes me love him even more. The answer he gives them is, "Because she is AMAZING."

Thank you, Jeff, for that answer. I love how pure my husband's love is for me. He's always telling me I'm a blessing to him, and how God saved him because of me. Truth be told, God knows how much I needed to be loved by someone—someone like Jeff.

Author's Note

Not only is my husband precious, he came from a loving and caring family. They welcomed me without judgement. Thank you for that.

Now I'm the mother of four wonderful children. Life is fun and crazy with driving them here and there. I'm very blessed to be close to family and grateful for my husband's parents' help in transporting some of our kids to their sports, dance, and all the other things kids do nowadays. And my kids are blessed to have three sets of grandparents who love and spoil them whenever they can.

I wish one day they would have the chance to go to Africa with me to see their other grandparents, too. The last time my husband and I went, they were still too small to come with us. Maybe when they grow a little older, they can. I am still concerned about safety in my country. When Jeff and I went, I worried about the war starting all over, but it was terrific seeing my family after twelve years. I pray for peace in Sierra Leone, so we can visit again.

I just wanted to say writing my story wasn't easy for me. So many times, I thought of making it into a book, but told myself no one would want to read it. Inside voices also said, *"Who do you think you are? You're not special or smart enough to do that."* So I put it off and tried not to think much about it. But whenever someone asks me about my story and I share it, they say I should write a book about it. I respond with a smile and say, "Maybe one day." But in my head, I knew I'd never do it.

After many years, I felt God calling me to write my story. I fought against it saying, *"But Lord, I don't want to. It hurts to go back and think of everything. I don't want to think of any of it. I just want to live my life the way it is right now and not dwell on the past.* Then I realized God wanted me to tell of Him. God is not selfish in asking me that. He is not a child who seeks attention.

I'm the one who is selfish. All I worried about were my feelings. I never gave a thought to how God has been with me every step of the way. I was given a story to tell, even when it wasn't that pretty to go through.

But the beautiful part is when God was in every moment fighting for me, when I couldn't fight for myself. I will never know *why* things happened the way they did, but I am happy God was with me.

So, I wrote my story, even though it was painful. I cried through half of it. Every time I wrote something, I relived the pain and hurt all over again. Sometimes I paused for a long time, and other times I just kept writing through my tears because I knew God wanted me to share it.

To be honest, life isn't fair to some of you. You may have been called a name that cuts deep. Or your parents never wanted you, so they gave you away. Maybe everywhere you go you can't seem to fit in, like you're the odd one. So you stop trying and want to give up everything—even the air you breathe. Please don't give up. I understand it can be very hard.

Sometimes, during my country's war, we lost hope. We didn't think anyone would make it, except for the rebels. I wanted to give up so badly, but I kept trying to stay alive. For what? I don't know, but God does.

After my first child, I faced a severe test of faith. I loved my little son very much, but how would I take care of him? I had to bathe him, dress him, pick him up, and carry him around without dropping him. All these activities seemed hard to do.

One day, my husband wasn't home to help me out. I undressed him for a bath. I thought that was the hardest part, but, oh, nooo, it wasn't. This baby was only three weeks old, so I couldn't ask him to help even a little.

While I watched this tiny, helpless baby look at me, I got on my knees and cried because I couldn't take care of him. I wanted this baby and didn't want to have to give him away just because I didn't think I could take care of him. I prayed to God for strength so I would be a mother to my child.

I took my Bible and read from Philippians. When I came to verse 4:13, it read like this: *"For I can do all things through Christ who strengthens me."* I love this verse. I repeated it over and over until I finished dressing him. From then on, I knew I could do all things in Christ who strengthens me.

So, I encourage you to find the verse that gives you strength in Christ Jesus, and be able to forgive freely.

Acknowledgements

I pray for God's abundant blessing on all these wonderful people, both mentioned and unmentioned, and their families.

Thank you to Mrs. Kathy J. Perry of Chickadee Words for helping me bring this book to life. I enjoyed every minute with you. Thanks for sharing funny videos with me and making me laugh. You are a great person to work with and I was so impressed with how quickly you understood my story and made it publish-ready. You did a lot of hard work in designing my website. Words cannot describe how grateful I am for you. Thank you again, from the bottom of my heart.

I want to give special thanks to the wonderful group of strangers who gathered in a room to pray for me in the Church of Nazareth. With only a picture of me, you kept praying for me without ceasing, and God heard you. When I arrived in the States, I was blessed to meet all of you and see the prayer room. God is amazing, and I'm so grateful for this group of godly people. I'll forever be grateful.

Matthew 18:20
"For where two or three gathered in my name, there am I with them." (NIV)

I would like to thank you, Dr. Schaffer, for all that you've done for me. Always ready and willing to do my surgery, you never asked for anything in return. Also, I thank you and your lovely family for always welcoming us into your home. I could never repay you for all you've done for me. I truly appreciate you and thank you very much for doing God's work.

I thank Grandpapa Louis Landry for always believing in me. You encouraged me to keep writing my songs and singing, and to never give up on writing my story. You took so much joy when reading my handwriting; something I wasn't too proud of. You encouraged me to love every little thing I do, even if it's not perfect. I feel proud when I accomplish things without hands, and I have you to thank for that. I loved that you introduced me to your beautiful families. Though you're not here today to read my book, like I wish you were, I know you'll be proud of me for finally getting it out there. I will always love you.

Words cannot describe how grateful I am with the many people that God has surrounded me with in my life. Each person in my life has played a very important role. Friends

I met from track were always there to help me when I needed help, especially one girl that I can never get away from, Debbie (lol). I love you Debbie. You are part of my family now, like it or not. Thank you for always being there. Although I don't ask for much, my friends and family are always there to support me. I am forever grateful for you all. I can't name everyone, because there are too many. We have eaten, laughed, prayed, and cried, and prayed some more together. You've welcomed me into your homes and invited me to get to know you. I am so blessed to have all of you in my life.

Thank you, Mom and Dad (aka Lonny and Katy Houk) for listening to God and traveling to a third-world nation, to feed the lambs of God. Thank you for all you've done and for saying yes to God. Being a missionary is hard work. In fact, it's very hard, scary, and can be dangerous. You said yes to something that you knew little about and put your life in danger. My country wasn't at peace yet from the war, but your saying yes to God means a lot. Sacrificing your life and leaving your family behind, without knowing what might happen to you, is a big step of faith. I'm thankful that God kept you safe and I'm blessed to be counted as a member your family.

Mama Shea, thank you very much for raising four girls by yourself. It wasn't easy dealing with hormonal girls and every day you worked hard to provide for us. You didn't have to take two more kids, but you did. I'm grateful for you and want to let you know you did a great job. Thank you for not losing faith, for helping us, and for always trusting God. I'll love you always.

Grandma and Grandpa Boyce, thank you for all your help, support, and for always being there to help drive the kids to their thousands of activities. You show up despite the rain or snow and I'm so grateful for you. I hope you know the dedication you show when you always put your grandkid first, even when you're sick. My kids are so lucky and blessed to have you in their life. Grandparents are very important in their grandkids' lives. I'm very thankful for mine, and so are my kids.

Thanks to all my teachers for taking the time to work with me and for your patience with my learning. English was not my first or second language, so it wasn't easy learning it or writing, but I'm grateful for all the help you gave. I'm still learning because the English language has so many words yet to be discovered. My next language to learn will be French. Bonjour!

And thank you to all those who encouraged me to write my story down. I did it! Thank you, Miss Kathy, for all your help and thank you to my husband for working with me and encouraging me to keep going.

Thank you to my Lord and Savior, my Redeemer. Jesus, I love you. Thank you for putting this story in my life to tell. Thank you for being there when my world was upside down, and for saving me. Thank you for fighting for me and for bringing caring, loving people into my life. Well, thank you for making me. I pray that my life would be a testimony to those who need encouragement in life. My story is not about me. It's about what you did for me, and I wrote this book for you.

And, lastly, to my children, I want you to never give up fighting or trusting and believing in God. Remember, God is always there. Just because you can't see Him, or you don't feel Him, that doesn't mean He's not there. And if you pray and your prayers go unanswered, don't give up hope. When your prayers take longer to answer, God is preparing a way for you. Never lose hope or faith in God. God is real. He is not fake.

I also pray that anyone who might be having a hard time believing in God will find hope in Him.

About the Author

I started life out as Isatu Kargbo in Sierra Leone, Africa. I enjoyed the first five years in my village: Moyamba. If it hadn't been for the violent civil wars caused by the rebels in the 1990s, I'd still live there, and my life would be very different from what it has become.

I wrote my story, even though it was painful. I cried through half of it. Every time I wrote something, I relived the pain and hurt all over again. Sometimes I paused for a long time, and other times I just kept writing through my tears.

Not only has my name changed over the years, but I lost both hands as a child during this war. But I came to realize that Jesus was with me the whole time. He gave me this story to share, and I thank Him for it.

I now live happily with my husband and four beautiful children in Missouri, USA.